Fifty Years to Shape a Dream:

1933-1983

By

Helen and Orville Strohl

Southwestern College Academic Press

100 College Street

Winfield, KS 67156

Printed in the United States of America

ISBN: 978-1-59831-001-6

Acknowledgements

This book was written in 1983 with great love, compassion and pride by our parents on their 50th wedding anniversary but is also a great chronology of Southwestern College from the founding in 1885 to the time of the Presidency of our father from 1954-1972. The jacket of the book contains important pictures of that era and comments from those folks our parents both respected and admired and we are honored for their contribution as well. We hope you enjoy reading it as much as we have enjoyed putting it together.

The Strohl family is thrilled with the publication of this book and we are sure our parents would be equally as excited. The project would not have been possible without the assistance of the Southwestern College Academic Press and the advice and counsel of Kristen Pettey and Dr. Kurt Keiser of the Southwestern College Business Division. Becky Pate of Sun Graphics was a wonderful director of the project.

Rod Strohl

Joanne Darfler

Sheryl Holt

Orville Strohl Remembered . . .

Dr. Strohl had a passion for international education that was evident to all, especially to the graduates of Southwestern College who were on campus for a year and then returned to Japan to live out effective careers. Mary Lou and I hosted the first alumni meeting in Tokyo, Japan. All those in attendance expressed deep gratitude to the Strohls and the Grays for all that was done for them.

Orville loved to start each convocation or event with the phrase, "It's a GREAT day for Southwestern." Because of an unusual sense of hopefulness and a passion for Southwestern College, he created many great days in my life and in the lives of many others. Because of his commitment many former students and graduates have lived in the world freed from fear, seeking knowledge and hope, and doing so with the courage to learn and live seeking excellence in service.

Dr. Carl Martin
Former President
Southwestern College

. . . .

When I think of Southwestern College and its excellence as a liberal arts college I invariably think of Dr. Orville Strohl. Through his outstanding and unique leadership he dramatically increased financial support and respect for the college.

Critically needed funds for the construction and maintenance of our extensive building agenda and support of the academic programs were somehow always made available by the friends of SC through his unique efforts and leadership.

His personal interest in the recruitment of excellent students and faculty members resulted in a truly exceptional learning environment enabling SC to become recognized as an icon of excellence and leadership among colleges of our size and mission.

One of the most unique strengths accompanying his tenure at SC was his wife, Helen, whose grace, elegance, intellect and warmth were shared and appreciated by everyone. Her ability to make guests of the college feel comfortable and welcome was extraordinary. I am sure she shared many constructive insightful thoughts concerning college operation and administration off as well as on the record.

Bob Wimmer
Emeritus Professor
Southwestern College

. . . .

Orville Strohl was the glue that held Southwestern College together after the disastrous Richardson Hall fire. Orville was the perfect President for the time and Helen was the perfect hostess. He was responsible for rebuilding the campus and Helen was responsible for entertaining the donors and trustees which she did perfectly.

Max Thompson
Emeritus Professor
Southwestern College

. . . .

It was 10:00 p. m. on the second Friday of September 1954 when Dr. Orville Strohl, the new president of Southwestern College (as of January 1954) called me and explained that there was an opening in the music department due to illness and would I consider applying for the position.

The last week of August I completed my master's degree and was contracted and teaching at Sublette, Kansas. My response to your father's offer was, "I am honored by the invitation and would be very interested, but I will not break my contract. However, I will discuss it with my superintendent and if he and the board will release me, I will apply."

A search was started and there was a young couple who had applied for two teaching positions. He was a cellist and she was a voice major. He was expecting the draft board to call him into service, but he took the job and sure enough, he was called up. His wife took over the job and did very well.

I applied and signed a contract with Southwestern to teach voice, music education courses, as well as supervising the senior music majors doing their student teaching, and directing a women's vocal ensemble.

Southwestern was into its third week of the semester when I arrived. Dr. Strohl knew very little about me but gave me my chance. He was an excellent mentor and very supportive of my work. Seven years later when I was offered a Fulbright lectureship in Colombia, S.A. to work with men's glee clubs in the universities of that country, Dr. Strohl made it possible for me to take a sabbatical from Southwestern and accept the Fulbright opportunity.

Dr. F. Joe Sims
Emeritus Professor
Southwestern College

"FIFTY YEARS TO SHAPE A DREAM"
A Reflection Upon Family Experiences

Written By

C. Orville & Helen Strohl
1709 Mound
Winfield, Kansas 67156
(On the occasion of their 50th wedding anniversary)

Cover By
Winfield Daily Courier
Winfield, Kansas

May 1, 1983

We express our deep gratitude to Rodney and Dorothy Strohl

for typing and duplicating this manuscript.

PART ONE

FIFTY YEARS TO SHAPE A DREAM

PREFACE

Behind every effort there must be a basic reason and he who reads
has a right to know the reason. Following is the reason for this story.

It is one thing to record the historical events of a family generation
with names, places and dates, but it is quite another task to try and add
the color, beauty and pathos of motivation, ideals, vision and insights
concerning struggle, courage, love and commitment. It is my hope that I
can do the latter. Visions do come to those who climb, and our family
has climbed.

Early in my ministry I found a poem that has meant much to me. I
refer to it below because it describes the attitude that has held us
together. This question is asked:

> "What is life?
> Is it dragging a load up a hill in a scorching light?
> Is it a faded rose?
> No!
> It is the magic of morning (youth and childhood)
> It is the glory of noontime (middle life)
> It is the wonder of nighttime (older years)
>   with their shadowy paths* to be trod,
> It is climbing from the valleys of men to the
>   windswept mountains of God."

Albert Camus in The Myth Of Sisyphus once said......
*"There is no sun without shadow, and it is essential to know
the night..... (When) a man says yes his efforts will be
unceasing..... The struggle toward the heights is enough to
fill the heart."

The Apostle Paul, whose life has always provided great inspiration
writes..... "Beyond what eye has seen and ear has heard, God has prepared
for those who love Him"(1 Cor. 2:9).

In those great experiences for which we could not find words to
express how we felt..... we knew that God was listening and that we were
heard (Idea in Romans 8:26-27). "In every life there are times when we
lift up our lanterns and it is not our flame that shall burn therein.
Empty and dark shall we raise them..... and the guardian of the night
shall fill them with oil and he shall light them also." (Idea from
The Prophet, by Kahlil Gibran).

From these points of view I write.....

FIFTY YEARS TO SHAPE A DREAM

ROOTS

STROHL-HAYWARD:

My father was the son of Joseph Strohl. He was born in Shelbyville, Illinois, on May 24, 1875. He died on July 16, 1941, at the age of 66 years. His sister Tempe was born there also on April 27, 1884. A second sister, Delight, was born in Barber County, Kansas, August 24, 1891. Joseph, my grandfather, was born in Perry County, Ohio, on February 14, 1844. He married Anna Mariah Kinnely. She was born in Westminister County, Pennsylvania, on August 11, 1850.

Joseph and Mariah came to Barber County, Kansas, in 1884 as pioneers in a covered wagon and lived on a farm until 1905. It was during these years that the Cherokee Run took place in 1893. They then moved to Medicine Lodge where they lived the remaining years of their lives. Medicine Lodge was an Indian settlement and got its name because this is where the medicine man resided. The annual observation of the founding of the town and the place the Indians played in it is a highlight in Kansas. My grandparents are buried in the Medicine Lodge Highland Cemetery. As you go North to Pratt, the stone near the highway can be easily seen. Joseph's wife died on November 13,1916, and his death followed on August 25, 1918, at 74 years of age. The local paper had an article announcing his death entitled, "Another Honored Citizen Gone". It reads, in part,

> "They were sturdy pioneers and had a large part in building up this new country. Aside from their busy, useful life, they were among our most active church workers and were always to be found uncompromisingly on the moral side of every question. Friends will always sacredly and proudly remember him as a strong-willed citizen, a true friend, and a man who always exemplified in his daily life the precepts of the Golden Rule as nearly perfect as it is possible for mortal man to do." (Original in file)

Mother's parents lived in Carlinville, Illinois. Her father's name was Morilus H. Hayward. He was born April 28, 1849 at Medora, Illinois. He was the second son of Ansel and Rebecca Hayward. The other children were Rothus (1846), Orville Eugene (1852) and John Franklin (1885). Morilus marries Eliza Robinson in 1879. They lived at Medora. Three daughters were born to this couple. Rose Hannah (1872), Ida Rebecca (1874), my mother, and Nellie May (1881). The family moved to Carlinville, 25 miles from Medora, in 1884.

The girls went to rural schools. Rose married a young farmer by the name of R.L. Barnstable. (There is a village on Cape Cod, Massachusetts named Barnstable. He was of English ancestry, and he and Aunt Rose visited England at one time). There is a town in California named Hayward for Uncle Orville Eugene Hayward. It is just South of Oakland with a population of 75,000. Eugene and I were named for him. My mother was very proud of him.

Rose and R. L. moved to Isabel, Kansas, a few years after their marriage, where he farmed. Ida went to visit her sister and helped during harvest. A young man from Medicine Lodge was hired to help also. His name was Clarence Strohl. Clarence and Ida were attracted to one another and soon fell in love. They both went to church on Sunday, which was held in the school house. It was the church and Sunday school parties that really got them together. Ida stayed there for a year.

Ida and Clarence were married on February 28, 1903 by Rev. Lahr, pastor of the church at Isabel. The marriage party all went to church that night! They lived on a tiny farm here for two years. Clarence was 28 years

of age and Ida 29 years when they married. He had joined the church when

he was 16 and Ida when she was 13.

> A Personal Word: My mother was a charming girl. What a sturdy
> character she had! She had a good mind but practically no
> opportunity to develop it in a formal way. And, what a heart she
> had! Dad was a good-hearted, loyal and dependable person. Not
> very handsome. His ears were large and he was an inch or two
> shorter than mother. But, they both knew how to work. They
> had dreams and hopes. I am so fortunate to look back
> upon those years with pride and joy and dedication. That was
> 80 years ago. Mother had ideals and vision. She had the
> business mind of the two. When I drive out through that part
> of Western Kansas I think about my great heritage and we have
> tried to pass it on to our children.

MEADE COUNTY

After two years this young couple agreed that they wanted a home

of their own. They planned carefully and the day finally came when they

headed West in a covered wagon. Ida's mother in Illinois thought she had

seen the last of her daughter forever! They went 200 miles West to Meade

County and staked a claim on 160 acres. It took them 5 days to make the

trip. They took 5 horses, 15 head of cattle, a saddle pony, 30 chickens,

and a very small amount of money! They arrived in August, 1905 and went

to work! It is my understanding that a woman who had started the claim

couldn't complete it. They paid the woman $300.00. She had a little

sod house and my parents stayed there until the one room frame house

was completed. The sod house was later used for chickens.

In 1910 they added two more rooms which served as a bed room and

living room. The original frame house was 12 by 14 feet, built by a

neighbor, Will Dalgran. The lumber came from Plains, 8 miles West. A barn, 16 by 32 feet was built. The first crop of wheat was in 1906.

I was born on Sept. 18, 1908 in that small room. When Dad called the doctor in Plains he said, "Mr. Strohl, do you have the money? I can't drive that far and not get paid." Dad had the money, so I came into the world, aided by a young physician whose name was Nickerson. Eugene was born June 7, 1910.

In 1906 my parents bought another quarter of land, and in 1914 a half section, making their holdings one section, 640 acres. The land was purchased from John Baughman of Liberal. The first quarter claim was granted by President William Howard Taft on May 20, 1905. The legal description was: the Northeast quarter of Section 9, township 32, South of range 29 West. The deed was issued at Dodge City.

Eugene's sickness, as an infant, was of great concern to my parents. He could not digest his food. Dr. Nickerson said there was no hope for him. Mother became a full time nurse all Summer, Fall, Winter and late Spring. They finally got food and medicine from a doctor in Medicine Lodge that began to make a difference.

I remember the Methodist Church at Plains so very well. At first it was driving 8 miles in horse and buggy, then our Model T Ford. The car dealer said to Dad, "Keep plenty of oil in it and if it will run without gas it will be O.K." Dad took him seriously. The result was that he flooded it with oil and we really had a problem.

Eugene and I attended a little rural school, a mile and a half from our home, known as District #30. I finished the 8th grade there.

It was during those years that I trapped skunks, assisted Dad with chores and did some field work driving teams of horses.

Dad saw me driving a nail into a shingle one day. He said, "Orville, use a smaller nail or the shingle will split". At another time he saw me using a plane of his on a 2 x 4. I was trying to plane against the grain. He said, "Orville, if you turn your board the other way it will work better". I did, and found he was right in both situations. Then I wondered how Dad could be so wise that he knew what would work and what would not work. In this way a child learns from his parents.

I have a very vivid memory of Mother saying to both Eugene and me that God always has a _purpose_ for life and that she was sure God had a purpose for each of us. It doesn't just suddenly come. One has to search for it, and find it, and follow it.

When I was in the 7th grade Dad took me to Meade, the county seat. By that time a new highway had been built through the hills East of us, and Meade was only 8 miles away. We transferred our membership from the church at Plains and started to do our banking at the First National Bank there. On that special day Dad took me into the bank to make a deposit; after that transaction he said, "Mr. Curl, this is my son, Orville" and lifted me up so I could shake hands through the cashier's window with the first vice-president and cashier of the bank. Then Dad told me to always find a banker who could be trusted and depend upon his word and advice. Then we went across the street to the Newspaper office and I met the editor and owner. Again, Dad said, "Always get the best news you can. Know what is going on". Good advice and I have never forgotten it.

I was about ten years of age when we were deeply involved in
World War 1. The slogan was "to make the world safe for democracy".
I can still see the long trains going through Plains with soldiers
hanging out windows waving to all of us. It made a very deep impression
on me. I later discovered that the world can never be made safe for
democracy. Democracy has to be <u>won</u> - it is a people's movement, always
changing and always up for grabs. Each generation must achieve democracy.

Those early years were full of memories. Art classes and socials
at the church in Plains that Dad would always take me to. I never
wondered what he did while he waited for me, but I do now! He'd work
all day in the fields, and then drive 16 miles round trip, <u>for me</u>.

I remember the minister called on us. Think of it! He came 8 miles
out from town. Before he left he opened his Bible and read the 1st Psalm.
I was probably 8 or 9 years old. How fitting it was to read that Psalm
to a farm family who had just completed harvest.

> "Blessed is the man that walketh not in the council of the
> ungodly..........etc."

> "He shall be like a <u>tree</u>" (and we had so few there on the
> windswept plains) "planted by the streams of water". Streams
> of water! We had none in Western Kansas! "That bringeth
> forth its fruit in its season; whose leaf also shall not
> wither, and whatsoever he doeth shall prosper." "The ungodly
> are not so, but are like the <u>chaff</u> which the wind driveth
> away." Chaff we knew, especially after harvest! It had no
> purpose but to be blown away. And I knew the strong winds
> in that part of the state would soon get rid of it.

The minister talked about that Psalm a bit and then had prayer with our
family. That is what I consider to be a pastoral ministry.

One day two men came to our little farm house and, after talking
to my parents for awhile Dad wrote a check and gave it to them. After they
were gone he said, "Orville, that check was to help our church college."

I couldn't figure that out. There wasn't any college in Plains or Meade. Years later I did understand. That was my introduction to Southwestern College!

Our windmill near the house provided us with the best cold water I have ever tasted. It was drilled in 1905. It was fun to climb up the ladder part way to the top. One day I was outdoors and heard a roar coming from the East. I climbed the ladder and saw my first single-engine airplane, heading West, and it went right over our house. When I was a senior in high school and working at Krogers Grocery Store on main street in Winfield, we all heard on the radio that Charles Lindberg had landed in Paris, making the first Trans-Atlantic flight. How I marvel at the fast growth of aviation.

At that store I was put in charge of the produce counter. I stacked bunches of carrots and celery, tops down. The manager came along and turned them, tops up. He said, "they get the customers attention this way." Breakfast foods that were not moving fast would be stacked in the aisles with preserves and jellies, suggesting breakfast. Getting the attention of the customer is the first principle of merchandising. It is still a good principle in any profession or vocation. I haven't forgotten those lessons and have used them in my work through the years.

In 1916 on the farm my parents built a large, hip-roofed barn to house the livestock and hay in the loft. I was required to learn to milk, and I mean required! This knowledge proved to be an advantage in later years.

A BIG MOVE FOR A GREAT PURPOSE

In 1922 my parents took a 4-day trip <u>without</u> my brother and me!
We stayed with neighbors, parents of our friends, Leonard and Kenneth
Shelman. We thought the folks were taking a little vacation. But I
soon learned that they were looking for a good community with a strong
educational program. They visited Pratt and Winfield. They chose
Winfield for its good high school and Southwestern College. When they
came home they told us that we would be moving in another year.

On April 9, 1923 Dad had a big farm sale. I remember so well
neighbors said, "Clarence, you are making a big mistake. Just at the
time when the boys are getting big enough to help you farm, you are
moving to town". Dad always replied, "Ida and I have something else in
mind". And they did! What was it? The education of their sons. What
vision they had. What sacrifices they were willing to make. They sold
the farm machinery, moved 250 miles to a town where we were not known. I
discovered they had arranged to buy a 5-acre tract at Cherry and 19th street
from a professor at St. John's College. It was at 1820 Cherry St. and
they paid $5,500.00 for it.

After the farm sale Dad and Eugene drove a good team hitched to a
covered wagon to Winfield. We left the farm the day after the sale.
Mother and I drove the Model T Ford, loaded to the limit. Mother never
learned to drive, so I did all of it: I was 14 years of age. It's
strange, but I do not remember a single experience of that trip. Did we
make in one day? What road did we take? When did we arrive? How long

did it take Dad and Eugene to get to Winfield? But I do remember Mother
and I arrived first, because I can still see the team and wagon coming
down Bliss Street headed South. What a move!

The very next Sunday we all went to church at First Methodist Church.
What a big church! A very beautifully dressed lady met us and shook hands
with each of us and welcomed us to her church. Wearing a big hat, gloves
and all kinds of jewelry she made quite an impression. She was Grace
Raymond, world traveler and famous artist. Let me say right here that I
was very, very self-conscious and really suffered when I had to meet
people, particularly strangers. That was the way I felt that first day at
church. But our family became great friends of Grace Raymond. There was
a world of difference in their station in life, but Miss Raymond was a
humble person, a fine Christian and very dedicated. For years she taught
Mother's Sunday School Class. And it's strange indeed that she became
one of my best friends, especially in later years when I became President
of Southwestern. I now have the easel which she used in painting all her
oils, and watercolors and we have four of her originals in our home, which
we purchased at the time of her retirement.

GROWING UP

The church meant much to us. After several weeks we all started to
Sunday School. My teacher was Curley Vaughn. That fall I unwillingly
agreed to start attending Epworth League. I always sat on the back row
and left early so I wouldn't have to talk to many. A year later I was
asked to lead the lesson. I agreed after much hesitation. I did it all

in 5 minutes! It was to have been 15 minutes, with discussion following.

I was so embarrassed I left immediately by the side door. As I walked

along on my way home I knew that I had failed but I said to myself "I

will do it again for Christ's sake and for my committment to Christ".

A very strong leader in our fellowship was a girl by the name of

Ruby Hill. She was known to dominate everything. In the Spring of my

Junior year she had been nominated to be President the following year.

Everybody seemed to agree that she would be elected. Down at the high

school a group of strong-minded Methodist youth didn't want her elected.

One day standing by my locker, they approached me and said, "We want

you to give us permission to nominate you for President". Well, I knew

I wouldn't be elected so I finally agreed with their argument that there

should be two nominees.

That bunch of kids really went to work and campaigned, not so much

for me as against Ruby just because they didn't want her to dominate

the program. The next Sunday night the election was held and I was elected.

What a schock! I became sick and scared. I got a little handbook written

by W. T. Kirkpatrick. I studied it, memorized it, and prayed over it.

Mother saw me eating less, losing weight and tried to help me.

Now I know that this experience and my high school class in debate

was God trying to lead me into self-confidence. I always prided myself

that my last name started with "S". In my first debate class in my Junior

year I was frightened but I thought that I would watch the first ones

whose names came before mine. When the class took up the teacher made

some opening remarks, analyzed the topic and then turned and called on

me! I stammered and I blushed.

What would I have done without the training that I received in my

youth fellowship and in my high school? I was called into the ministry and later into college administration where I had to approach people, many strangers and hard 'nuts' to crack; where I had to speak, preach, persuade and argue for my convictions. God does really work through all things for good to those who love Him. (Romans 8:28) And of course, that is what a youth fellowship and a high school class is all about.

That Spring, all of the officers of the Epworth League were publicly installed on a Sunday evening at Church. It was a candle lighted service. At the close we all presented ourselves at the altar and Rev. D. W. Switzer (1927-30) shook hands with each of us and made a statement to each one. He said to me, "Orville, remember it is the man who honors the office and not the office that honors the man". I remember that so vividly and it has followed me all through life- and most vividly at the college level. I respected the office to which I had been called and installed. But it is easy for a person to disgrace an office and diminish it by being willing to exploit it for one's own ego.

Years later (1962) the church building was razed to make room for a new sanctuary. The Rev. Forrest Robinson was the minister and a good friend of mine. In conversation with me one day, during this demolition period, I said to him, "Forrest, I have a request to make of you." "What could that be?" he said. "I would like to have 3 feet of the church alter and I'll tell you why. Years ago, 39 years to be exact, I stood at that alter and joined the church. There is where I started my first elected position in the Epworth League. There is where I knelt with my parents and my brother and took communion. It's a sacred alter and I would like to have a small section."

A few days later he brought it. Henry Murray put ends on it. I
have it in a spot in our home where I can see it and use it regularly.
Always one will find a Bible on it and a good book or two. It links me
with the past involving my family, my church, and my faith.

There were other experiences in high school that were very meaningful
to me. We had a guest speaker one day in my sophomore year. We had all
assembled in the auditorium. I had come from a French class. Among
other things he said, "That which you are to become, you are now in the
process of becoming." I copied that statement on the back page of my
French book and looked at it again and again. When I got home I looked
at myself in the mirror. What did I see? I was not handsome; I was really
ugly. What I was to become..... I was then in the process of becoming!
Really? Boy, I had a long way to go. I got a new perspective of myself.
It was a decisive moment for me. Maybe that is "growing up. Is it possible
that some young people never have those schocking moments?

Some good friends of my parents, whose name was Driver, lived on
7th street and visited our home often. One day Mrs. Driver said to me,
"Orville, you are going to make it because you listen, respond to
suggestions, and are responsible." Someone beyond my parents was
expressing confidence in me. We must do this for the young!

For years I have made it a practice to speak to the young and
children of all ages. I have paid attention to my grandchildren. Walks
with Kirk, and Chad, swinging with Elizabeth and the "crooked finger"
with Brian and Chad. I've written letters and notes to all our grandchildren and will continue to do so. When my time comes to end my
earthly pilgrimage, I want my grandsons to assist carrying my casket
to its final resting place. They are, and will continue to be, the
pride of our lives.

My parents purchased a piano - a small one - and Eugene and I started taking piano lessons. It didn't last long, but I do remember being in a recital. I learned to read notes and developed a sense of rhythm. Then, C.O. Brown, our high school band instructor, urged my folks to start both of us on instruments. Eugene started with the French Horn, a very hard instrument to play, and I started with a cornet. I finally purchased a King Trumpet, with purple-lined carrying case. I played in the high school and college bands a total of 6 years.

In 1925 we moved to 1214 Broadway. We sold the team that Dad had kept while on the acreage. When I finished high school the folks bought a residence at 901 East 6th, paying $5,200.00 for it. They lived there for 11 years and then moved back to Broadway. This is the location of my fathers sudden death by heart attack on July 16, 1941, at 8:30 a.m.

Clinton Swengel became associate minister of our church in 1927. He came from Nebraska Wesleyan, was a fine singer, and was energetic and young. He became a real companion. During my freshman year at Southwestern I was elected president of the Winfield District Epworth League. This included five counties. The other officers came from Belle Plaine, Wellington, etc. This was good experience and I made some life long friends.

SOUTHWESTERN COLLEGE

College days, from 1927-1931, were a time of growing. I became a member of the Athenian Society and the Brown Derbies, a pep group. In my senior year I was elected business manager of the Moundbuilder, our college yearbook. Money was difficult to raise that year, but we made it, raising $5,000.00 from advertising.

I developed a double major, sociology and biology. My majors were taught by two of the greats! Ada Herr in sociology and Dr. William Goldsmith in biology. These majors fit beautifully into my chosen vocation which I decided on in my junior year.

There are 3 great decisions that every person must make: (1) his profession (2) his life style and (3) the person he is going to marry. Any one of these makes a powerful plus or minus in a person's life. Here is where the dream starts! How simple! How silently the decisions are made. Slowly the blessings are realized.

(1). The decision I made to give my life to God that he might become a little more real-expressed through the ministry of the Methodist Church- was the right decision for me. I have always felt that God could take the simplest ways of men and clothe them in beauty and grandeur. Little people can become great if they will link their lives with His.

(2). This required that I make a personal decision to be a follower of Christ. Those who do so find in Christ "the way, the truth, and the life." Start walking in the way, follow sincerely the truth and we experience the life.

(3). I married the right girl. It wasn't all clear from the beginning for either of us. It was a long engage- ment---educational plans had to be completed---distance of miles stood between us---but on June 14, 1933 we linked our lives for better or worse. Helen has been a great companion in our personal lives, in our professional responsibilities, in our church relationships and in our social and family life. She is sensitive to people and responds to music and color and grandeur as one who apprec- iates the work of the hand of God.

All dreams start with these 3 choices.

In March of my Sophomore year I was driving home from the downtown area in Winfield. Money was scarce in those days, and students learned to wait til the bus left the bus stop, then go to the corner of McGregor's Hardware

store and the few students lucky enough to have cars would gladly take
'passengers'. I had a Ford roadster with a rumble seat and was on my way
to the campus. I saw two coeds--recognized one of them, so stopped. She
was Lillie Mahoney and her roommate, Helen Burgner. The next day, Ted
Hawkins, also a Sophomore, and I decided to get dates and go to the theater
in Ark City. Ted had a girl, but I did not. Being adventuresome I said
I'd call my friend Lillie and ask her if I could get a date with her roommate. I talked to Lillie. She thought Helen would be interested, so I
asked her to tell Helen I would be calling back in a few minutes. I did
that, and without too much persuasion, Helen agreed to go with me!

I dated many other girls, but it was Helen who somehow made a lasting
impression upon me. The year was 1928. Who was this Freshman who made
such an impression on me? Helen attended elementary and high school at
Rolla, Kansas, a small town of about 500 people. The high school was
about 50 students, and there were seven Seniors in the class of 1927.
There was a home economics teacher who made a great impression on Helen.
She had graduated from Southwestern College, and that was Helen's decision
too. Genevieve Godding became Helen's ideal, and she could talk to the
parents and give them some firsthand information about the school.

Helen graduated from high school when she was 16 years of age. Her
birthday in November would make her 17, but her father thought she was too
young to go to college! So, she worked part time in the office of the
superintendent of schools, took two courses in business. She did date some...
mostly the young man who had come to Rolla to be principal of the Grade school.
She also worked some at the store her father and uncle owned...Russell and
Burgner, General Merchandise Store. The Burgner family was active in the

18

Methodist Church. Helen sang in the choir, attended church school and church regularly. While Oscar Matthews was minister at Rolla, the laymen made the brick for a new building. "To us it looked like a Cathedral". Helen has said, but it really was quite small and was replaced in the 1970's by a new brick structure. It was a heartbreak, really, for us to see the old building fall, brick by brick. Friends wished they would tear it down.

It was the Fall of 1928 that Helen came to Southwestern, riding with Henry Gerber and Lurline Weitzel who also enrolled that Fall. Here in Winfield on McGregor's corner, 9th and Millington is where our paths crossed for the first time a few months after school started. For two years we were together and grew fond of each other as time went on.

In the Summer of 1929 I got a job working for a young farmer South of Johnson; they lived in a sub-basement home. On one weekend I borrowed his car and drove to Rolla. I found the Burgner residence and Dad Burgner was out in front supervising the laying of a sidewalk. He had just received word of a death in his family and he and Mother were going to have to go to Texas. Helen and I drove to Grandmother Russell's farm, about 15 miles South of Rolla, and brought her back to stay with the 'clan'. Helen and I drove to Elkhart for supper (it must have been a dilly) and I stayed in the Rolla Hotel that night. It left much to be desired! In the meantime I continued my college education. I became the President of the Senior class. Our gift to the college was 300 feet of concrete sidewalk, to be placed on the South side of the circle drive extending to College Street. I remember making a miniature of the sidewalk to present to the

19

President at our final assembly. A small plaque was laid into the walk which read "Gift from the Class of 1931". By strange coincidence, for over 18 years (1954-1972) I drove over that sidewalk going in and out of the garage at the President's new home at 110 College! And I walked on it all those years back and forth to my office in Christy administration building.

It was in my College Junior year that I made my decision for the Christian ministry. I remember the time and place that the decision was made. A very quiet, conscious and deep committment. Roy L. Smith was speaking at Vespers at the foot of the 77 steps. Topic, "Plowing The Sea With Oxen".

I served for 6 months the church at Beaumont, a railroad town 60 miles from Winfield. Then I was assigned to Palestine, North of Oxford. Just before I left for graduate school I served Grandview for a few months.

I went to Denver in the early Summer of 1931 immediately after graduation from Southwestern, and entered Summer school. Mother was very quiet at breakfast that morning, but she served me strawberries! She knew that once a son left home he was really leaving for good. It was a tender moment for our family.

Meanwhile the Burgners moved from Rolla, Kansas, to Boulder, Colorado in August of 1930. Our romance continued however and was kept alive by daily letters and holiday visits. When I accepted a scholarship at Iliff Graduate School, the president, Dr. Cutshall, thought I chose the school for the 'huge' scholarship. He didn't know Helen was at Boulder! She has been shaping my life ever since! Helen brought a long line of heritage to be interwoven with mine.

20

BURGNER-RUSSELL

William Russell, Helen's grandfather, was born on May 4, 1839, in
Ireland. He came to the United States with his parents when he was 3
years of age. His father worked on ships, so probably worked for their
passage. They settled in Kentucky. One day his father had to make a
trip up the river and his mother wanted to accompany him for the day.
They had been here such a short time that they hardly knew their neighbors,
but they left William with them for the day and took the baby. There
was an explosion on the boat and all were killed. There was little choice
for the neighbors; they already had a large family, but they had to
keep William. It was an unhappy experience for him, and as soon as he
could, he ran away, probably to Kansas. Whenever his foster mother
tried to punish him, he would run to the blackberry patch where she
couldn't get to him. One of the girls in the family kicked him in the
shins and he vowed that when he had a family of his own there would be
no kicking. That's a vow he always kept. He enlisted in the Civil
War, near its end, and while he was gone his fiance died.

In 1872 several families living in Indiana came by covered wagon
to Kansas. There wasn't room for everyone to ride, so they all took
turns walking. Ida Mohler, Helen's grandmother, did her share of
walking on that trip. She was born on June 14, 1869. They lived first
at Lane, Kansas, and then moved to Rantoul. When she was 18 years of
age, she married Wyatt Atkins (1887) but he died six weeks later of
typhoid fever. In 1888, on February 29, she married William Russell.
Six children were born:

21

Pearl May - February 2, 1889
William Leonard - October 8, 1890
Floyd Alexander - December 31, 1898
Bessie Anne - November 5, 1897
Otis Sterling - March 22, 1901
James Shirley - May 14, 1904

All these children are gone now, except for Pearl, who is 93 years of age; we're looking forward to celebrating her 94th birthday in 1983!

Pearl married Charles Swatzell Burgner on December 16, 1909. Charles was born in Chuckey, Tennessee, on August 31, 1884, the son of Peter and Mary Burgner. His mother died in 1886 and his father in 1893. He went to live with an aunt and uncle, Ike and Callie Newberry. They were also from Tennessee, but moved to Brownsville, Texas.

Charles proved up a claim in Texas County, Oklahoma, when he was 21 years of age. By that time the William Russell family had also come to Texas County and bought a relinquishment of a claim. It was here that Pearl and Charles met, at an old fashioned box supper in a school house. They were married in 1909 and lived in the far West end of the Oklahoma panhandle. In 1915 they moved to Rolla, Kansas. They had four children:

Helen Lillian - November 29, 1910 at Camp, Okla.
William Vernon - September 9, 1913 at Camp, Okla.
Charles Russell - August 12, 1915 at Camp, Okla.
Noma Lora - April 29, 1920 at Rolla, Kansas

Here then is a brief sketch of the Strohl-Hayward and Burgner-Russell heritage, reaching back to 1839. I record these names and dates so they will be preserved and give us an appreciation of our pioneer background. It also becomes a foundation upon which someone in the future may wish to add their chapter.

22

DENVER, COLORADO

While a student at Iliff School of Theology I served as a student
pastor in Central City. At one time, Central City was the capitol of
Colorado. It had great prosperity in the early days and the church
is a beautiful building with a great pipe organ and a sanctuary that
would seat 500 people. I lived on weekends at the Teller House Hotel.

One year later I was appointed to a small church on the West edge
of Denver, called Barnum. For years, the Barnum and Bailey Circus
management kept their livestock there during the summers. That is
where the name came from. And I might add, that little church
provided me with excitement comparable to that of a circus. I was
serving that church when Helen and I decided to get married. We were
determined not to get married until she had finished her work at Colorado
University. (I might say that her father had something to say about
that also.) She graduated on the 12th of June and we were married on
the 14th of June. I had the marriage license in my pocket when I sat in
Mackey Auditorium and watched Helen get her diploma.

It was our plan to be married in Boulder in the Methodist Church,
her home church. When I announced our plans to my small congregation
and the youth, who had been very active, they pleaded with me to be
married in their church. They said they would paint the church, provide
flowers, decorate and arrange for the reception, etc. Everybody was
willing and so we changed. Helen's minister, the Rev. Oscar Beckman,
came to Barnum to perform the wedding.

23

A STORM IN THE ROCKIES

I must not omit a terrifying experience that took place in the winter of 1932. My closest friend in the ministry and my roomate was Frances Brush. He served the church at Idaho Springs, near Central City. I had gone to Central City on Friday, taking another close friend by the name of Birney Roberts, who was going to preach for me. Frances was engaged to Helen Nelson of Denver. They went through Boulder and picked up Helen Saturday evening. The five of us were planning a wonderful Sunday. When they left Boulder the weather was beautiful. But, Central City was in the midst of a horrible snow storm. When it hit, I called Boulder but they had already left. Birney and I waited until 2 p.m. and there was no sign of them. So we prepared for the worst. Dressed in heavy snow clothing, we got our car out of a warm garage and started down that steep and rugged canyon toward Netherlands. Slowly we crept down, looking over steep canyons for some trace of a car. After traveling some 40 or 45 miles, we found an abandoned car in the ditch, covered with blown snow. Exploring, we found no one in the car, but it did belong to Frances. We sounded our car horn and yelled. Finally we saw a tiny evidence of smoke above the pines, against the early morning light. As we walked in that direction we saw Frances walking toward us, but in snow nearly four feet deep.

They had found a miners cabin, pushed open the door, found a tiny stove and wood, and kept warm in the blizzard. They were found, and what a happy reunion we had! We managed to get back to Central City and put the girls to bed, while the rest of us preached at our 2 communities, Central City and Idaho Springs. Then came together for dinner at the old historic

24

Teller House. Incidentally, the girls slept in the bed and the room in
which President U.S. Grant had slept years before.

WHY WE DIDN'T RETURN TO KANSAS

It is natural for one to ask why we didn't want to return to Kansas.
I was well known in Kansas because of my activity in the conference,
mentioned earlier. That was one reason why I did not want to return. I
have never been wild in my desire to adventure but somehow I wanted to get
a new and fresh start. I did study conference journals, state maps, and
other background materials. If we started in a brand new conference and I
fell on my face and became a dud, I would have no one to blame but myself.
(My uncle, referred to in Part 1, whose name was R.L. Barnstable, was now
a Methodist minister in Iowa and he recommended we move there.) If I had
reasonable success, it would be entirely on my own. In other words, I had
to choose between the "terrible No and Yes". As I now write, I am sure
that if we had returned to Kansas I never would have been given the opportunity to become the president of Southwestern College. By being away
for 20 years and serving under 4 bishops and many district superintendents,
I developed a positive image. I quote from a letter that Bishop Brashares
sent to Rev. Joe Riley Burns, who was pastor of First Methodist Church of
Winfield, dated January 18, 1947. Brashares had been invited to come to
Kansas to speak and had to decline. He said, " Especially would I like to
come to an interdenominational situation such as you have outlined, and
especially would I like to come and tell the people of one whom they have
helped to produce ---- C. Orville Strohl ---- who is, we believe, one of the
best in the field of Christian education. What he is accomplishing in this
area is marvelous beyond words".

25

AN INVITATION LINKING 1982 WITH 1933

In November of 1982 the telephone rang. "Denver calling," the operator said, " my party is asking for Rev. Strohl". Helen called me to the phone. I have been given many titles, but the title "Reverand" indicated an older person and one who had known us some time ago. The voice said, "This is Julia Willis, Julia Thomilson Willis". Sure, I remembered. I had married Julia and Melvin one week after Helen and I were married on June 14, 1933.

She was inviting us back to our student church to preach for their 75th anniversary. It had long ago become a full time appointment and had changed its name to Bethany. So, on January 31, 1982 we were there and I stood at the very spot where I was married 50 years earlier, and where I had learned the art of church administration and the importance of preaching. A lot of the congregation were the former youth. After church, a beautiful reception was held in our honor. That's the way we started celebrating our 50th wedding anniversary. I had not seen, nor had I written the Willises since we left Denver in 1934. They knew where we were and how to reach us. For Helen and myself this was a very significant invitation and we will always be thankful to Julia and Melvin Willis. Many of our immediate family were present.

PART TWO

26

PART TWO

OUR MOVE TO IOWA - CARLISLE

I had rented a small apartment on University Boulevard, across the street from Denver University. I had one more year in graduate studies. I had spent a lot of time and study as to where we were going to start our full time ministry. I did not want to return to Kansas. I was invited to go to Wyoming and Nebraska. But really, the size of Iowa was impressive. I knew that there had to be a lot of churches of all sizes if we were to have an opportunity to advance. Iowa had 300,000 Methodists. Wyoming's population was less than the population of Denver and I knew that peoples style of life in Wyoming was much different from that in Iowa. And certainly they were not all Methodists.

OUR BEGINNING IN IOWA

In September of 1932 we went to Des Moines, expecting to join the conference on trial. Bishop Leete would not accept anyone, so I was accepted in 1933 in absentia. In September of 1934 we attended our first annual conference at Burlington and I was ordained Deacon by Bishop Waldorf. We were assigned to Carlisle, a small town 12 miles from Des Moines. The Bishop asked several of us to take two minutes and tell the conference why we were joining that conference. I remember that I said, among other things, that I had just been assigned to the greatest church in that conference and I was anxious to get started and, of course, I wanted to be a member of that conference. As a matter of fact, the members of the congregation in Carlisle had voted, just before conference, not to have a minister. They didn't think they could pay for one. I didn't know that. After I made that little talk, several ministers

came around and asked me where I had been assigned. (Every church is a great church because it has a great Christ, a great message and a great fellowship). Our district superintendent was Raymond M. Shipman. The salary was to be $800.00 annually and an unfurnished parsonage.

That first evening we were to have supper with Roy and Ida Thomas. They lived near the church and were the "salt of the earth". He was the director of the only funeral home in town. About a mile outside of Carlisle we stopped and I put on a coat and combed my hair, and Helen used her lipstick. A car passed us and later we discovered that they were active members of our congregation and they were sure that we were their new pastor and his wife. When we drove into the driveway of the parsonage it was raining. It was September 18, my birthday. It had not rained there all summer. The minister I followed was the Rev. Van Dyke. He had planted a big garden early in the Spring and when it didn't come up, he planted one in June and repeated it again in July and then in August. It wasn't long before I had the funniest garden in town.... four months all in one....when everything came up. We all started growing at the same time!

We went to Des Moines and purchased enough furniture to start housekeeping. We made a payment and the rest on monthly installments. That was our first real home and our first full time church. I started to learn. Example: a very strong minded older woman objected to some changes that we were making. She came to me. I said, "that was the decision of the committee," and it had been. Committees protect individuals and that is their purpose. She could take me on, but not the whole committee. It was here that a young man decided to enter the ministry

under our leadership. His name was Glenn Lamb, who, after a number
of years of study, became a very effective minister and who is still
one of our very best friends. I later married Glenn and Merle, who
lived in West Des Moines, on the day before Joanne was born. Dr. James
Brett Kenna, pastor of the large Methodist church in Des Moines, had
been in Wichita when I was in college. He had moved to University Temple
in Seattle and now was in Des Moines. I made an appointment with him
and told him how new I was and that I wanted to know more about preaching.
I wanted to know how to keep notes on books that I would read, how to
plan for long-range sermon preparation, etc. I will always remember
that I sat and talked to him for over an hour and he never really gave
me a single good idea. I will always suspect that he did not have a
plan. But one thing that I did learn was that all the men who were at
the bigger appointments were not necessarily there by merit and that a
young man who worked and had a plan did have a chance. Isn't it strange
how negative experiences sometimes work out to be positive influences?

Every young minister was soon to be asked to serve in summer camps
and Institutes. I was asked. Older men didn't always have the time or
did not want to. At a training conference in preparation for a summer
institute on the campus at Simpson College a young man by the name of
Lloyd Tennant from Green Castle, Indiana, came to be the leader of several
sessions. He was to talk to us about being CREATIVE, IMAGINATIVE, &
CHALLENGING. That's what I wanted to be. I took notes and followed his
suggestions for years and hope that I profited from his leadership. I am
sure that the effort to be creative...helped me greatly in my ministry
and in the work of the college. John Lennon, who was not a Christian,

September 24, 1935

Reverend and dear Sir:

　　　　Your high calling brings you into intimate
daily contact not only with your own parishioners,
but with people generally in your community. I am
sure you see the problems of your people with wise
and sympathetic understanding.

　　　　Because of the grave responsibilities of
my office, I am turning to representative Clergymen
for counsel and advice,- feeling confident that no
group can give more accurate or unbiased views.

　　　　I am particularly anxious that the new
Social Security Legislation just enacted, for which
we have worked so long, providing for old age pensions,
aid for crippled children and unemployment insurance,
shall be carried out in keeping with the high purposes with which this law was enacted. It is also
vitally important that the Works Program shall be
administered to provide employment at useful work,
and that our unemployed as well as the nation as a
whole may derive the greatest possible benefits.

　　　　I shall deem it a favor if you will write
me about conditions in your community. Tell me where
you feel our government can better serve our people.

　　　　We can solve our many problems, but no one
man or single group can do it,- we shall have to
work together for the common end of better spiritual
and material conditions for the American people.

　　　　May I have your counsel and your help?
I am leaving on a short vacation but will be back in
Washington in a few weeks, and I will deeply apprec-
iate your writing to me.

　　　　　　　　Very sincerely yours,

　　　　　　　　Franklin D Roosevelt

Reverend C. O. Strohl,
Carlisle, Iowa.

was an effective singer because of his use of Imagery. Use ideas....
make them stick....by using imagery....and dramatic ways of expressing
thoughts and experiences and ideas.

Our first baby was born while we were at Carlisle. A heavy snow
storm had swept into the State and that weekend the roads were banked high
with snow drifts. I was at church preaching when a neighbor came to the
back of the sanctuary and indicated that I was needed. I dismissed the
service in a hurry and made for the parsonage. Helen and I were soon
on our way to the Iowa Methodist Hospital in Des Moines. That was Sunday,
January 31, 1937. That baby was born on Monday morning, February 1, at
about 1:30 a.m. We named her Sheryl Jeanne.

MADRID

In the Spring of that year a car drove up to the parsonage and 3
men came to the door. They were Roy Neff, Earl Brown and Walter Anderson
from Madrid. Sheryl was a baby in Helen's arms. They needed a new and
young minister at their church and wanted to know if we would move to
Madrid after Conference. Well, what a compliment! And how would we handle
it with the Bishop and two District Superintendents? It was handled and
we did move to Madrid the end of that third year. We thought we were on
the way and we were.

It was at Madrid that Joanne was born on May 28, 1941. Again, it
was at Iowa Methodist Hospital. I took Helen to the hospital, and then
went to perform the wedding of Glenn and Merle Lamb at West Des Moines
Methodist Church. Dad and Mother came to take care of the family while
Helen was in the hospital. A few days after Helen got home, the folks

journeyed back to Kansas. Mother forgot her black purse. We discovered
it after about fifteen minutes so I got in the car and overtook them
about 20 miles on their way. For some reason it was a very emotional
meeting, which lasted only four or five minutes. That was the last time
I saw my father alive. He died six weeks later on July 16. On my way
to his funeral, driving by myself, I reflected deeply upon his life.
Find in the appendix of this document my article, "Asleep In His Chair."
We were in Madrid for five years. The church was able to purchase a
pipe organ which was in a theater that was being torn down. I had
designed a grill that was to cover the pipes, and Earl Brown made the
grill. Some of those pipes were as "soft as butta (butter)" was the
remark of the fine old gentleman who installed the organ. Helen had the
thrill of being church organist, which was the only time she was to have
the opportunity. She had taken organ lessons from Mrs. Ira Morton, whose
husband was on the faculty at Iliff. She was a good church organist.
We used the chapel organ at Iliff.

Madrid was a coal mining town located 25 miles North of Des Moines,
and it was 15 miles from Boone, the county seat. It was 20 miles from
Ames, where Iowa State College was located. The three men who had come
to Carlisle to ask us to move, stood behind us through those five years
of our ministry at Madrid. They were also life long friends. Walter
Anderson is the only one still living.

One of the real highlights of my pastorate there was an invitation
to lead the Morning Watch sessions at the conference institute at Simpson
College. These were the inspirational services for the entire group.
They were very important because they set the tone for the rest of the day.
I prepared printed programs and used many of the young people to assist.

31

NEW LONDON

Our third church was at New London, near Mt. Pleasant. That's the
home of Iowa Wesleyan College and the birthplace of the P.E.O. Sisterhood.
Helen joined that organization in 1938 in Madrid. There had been two
Methodist churches in New London, Methodist Episcopal and Methodist
Protestant. In 1939 there was a uniting conference in Kansas City,
Missouri, which merged the two churches in New London. But it took time
to salve feelings and so it was our job to see that everyone was happy
and that it was a smooth transition. One of the funeral directors
purchased the Methodist Protestant building and converted it to a funeral
chapel, which helped a great deal. I followed an older minister there
who was a very good preacher, so my work was cut out for me there, as
it had been in the other churches. Our salary was $1,500.00 that first
year. It had gone as high as $1,300.00 in Madrid!

Churches settle down just like other institutions and need a storm
once in awhile to stir up the marine life that has settled to the bottom.
I had attempted a district meeting where a Methodist layman spoke. He
was the district manager for the Des Moines Register, a statewide newspaper. He said, "Men, let me compare my work to the work of you ministers.
I have to be RED HOT all the time about my job because the carriers with
whom I work are LUKEWARM about what their responsibilities are, and the
public is ICE COLD." That inspired me to apply the same principle to
my work in the church through the years. There were few 'new' members.
There was a very small youth group, and we needed MEN. So I suggested
to the official board that we set aside a Sunday to receive MEN ONLY.
That was an impossible dream! But they did agree to set a date and help

with the effort. When that day arrived, we had 22 men join the church,
some of them on Confession of Faith, and three were baptized who were over
70 years of age. The church was full. Families were there. Wives sat
with moist eyes. God was at work in our congregation that Sunday!

Helen and I decided that we were going to try to win youth in the
community. We went to the Senior play at the high school and saw the
talent those young people had....in acting....in music....and other ways.
I found out that after school they made a bee line for the drug store for
candy bars and cokes and fun. So after that I was there at 4:00 o'clock
and began to get acquainted. One day a young woman who worked there,
Margaret Westerbeck, pulled out a White Owl cigar and stuck it in my
handkerchief pocket of my coat; two inches of it showed. When I left
the store I forgot it, and I made some calls on downtown business men.
When I got home, Helen saw it right away and wondered how a thing like
that could have happened. She was embarrassed for me, but it turned out
to be just a good-natured joke! The next Sunday my congregation knew all
about it!

We started the program for youth by inviting a Youth Caravan....a
group sponsored by the Youth Department of the General Board of Education.
They were trained in several areas, and then sent out in teams of 6 or 7
and were accompanied by an adult. The Caravan was effective. Before they
left we had over 70 in attendance. One of their members, Aletha Vogel,
returned that Fall to be our youth director and enrolled at Iowa Wesleyan.
And that year also, we had 10 members of our church attend Iowa Wesleyan.
Let me quote from my Fourth Quarterly Conference Report, December 14, 1944:

"The youth caravan arrived on July 31 and spent one week with us.
It ended with a beautiful out-of-door communion service at the Country

33

Club Lake. At the close each of the 100 people attending placed their lighted candle on the lake. A beautiful sight! No funds were drawn from the treasury because we planned for it to be self-supporting. It was a week remembered as being one of the highlights of our work with youth."

I reported on May 1, 1943 that we had received 45 members into the church, 17 of them on Confession of Fairth. Thirty baptisms were administered. Let me say with deep conviction that I become impatient with ministers who say today that they can't reach youth - they can't increase the church school, etc. Of course it takes work, but it can be done because it is a part of the work of the Kingdom of God. I decided that no Methodist minister ever needed to fail because we are a connectional church and can reach out for any kind of special help we need. In the year of 1943 we had 12 outstanding persons as guest resource persons in our church....including women who represented Methodist Women....missions in South America, India, China....representatives of the general board of education for our church and also in higher education and others.

We were in New London during the war and Iowa Wesleyan was training Air Cadets. We entertained some of these young men in our church on Sundays. Again I quote: "We had 25 cadets the first Sunday....and 33 the second time. They were here for church, had dinner in the homes of our members and we took their pictures with their hosts and sent them to their parents." Nothing like this had been done before. We heard from some of their parents.

Here, also, Rodney was born to take his place in the Orville and Helen Strohl family. I had a funeral the morning Helen felt 'called' to go to the hospital at Burlington, so Ruth Cornick took her over

icy roads. (If we had served 15 churches, we might have had 15 children.) I was able to get to the hospital before Rodney arrived and when the Doctor announced to me "It's a boy" I said, "Now, I have a boy." The date was November 25, 1944.

The Raymond Cornicks had become very close friends of ours. Early in our ministry there at New London I called on all of our church members. Helen enjoyed going with me most of the time. It was about 4:30 one afternoon when we stopped at the Cornicks. They lived about 3 miles from town. We visited for a while and then Mr. Cornick jumped up and said, "It's chore time and I have to go and milk." He grabbed two buckets and handed me one. I followed him to the barn. The cows were in their stalls. He gave me a three legged stool and pointed to a young cow. (He told me later that she was the hardest of the ten to milk). I sat down and milked about a half a bucket, and then getting up said, "Which one next?" Thanks to my farm experience, I was able to turn his bluff into a life long friendship. He thought I was a city kid and totally inexperienced in farm life. Raymond was a man of great talents, a good farmer, later became our State Representative, a trustee of Iowa Wesleyan College and an effective leader in our church.

President Stanley Niles, President of Iowa Wesleyan, invited me to teach a 3 hour course each semester, rotating between religion, philosophy and logic. It was a great challenge and I worked hard. I taught courses for two years. It was a source of extra money and gave me exposure to a new group of people.

35

Frank Lindhorst was executive secretary of the Iowa Commission on Christian Education of the Methodist church. His office was in Des Moines but he traveled the state. His work was supervised by an Area Commission comprised of representatives of the three annual conferences. He resigned from the Iowa position to go to California to teach on the college level. For a reason I will never know, I was recommended to replace him. I could not see us moving to Des Moines, and for me to live out of a suit case and a brief case. It would mean working with 14 District Superintendents (one had always seemed sufficient to me), nearly 900 ministers, many laymen, youth in summer camps and other educational projects. I was too nicely situated, with a church and a part time teaching position in a Methodist college. It took 3 months for us to agree to make the change. Bishop Brashares was very insistant....he thought that I was the one and only. But I remembered that sometimes when God seems far off He is often close at hand through a friend. Brashares was a loyal friend.

These 3 experiences were so pivotal in our growth and development. Reflect for a moment on the highlights:

Carlisle: Sheryl was born.
Glenn Lamb decided for the Christian Ministry.
Three strong laymen from Madrid sought us to be minister.

Madrid: Installing a new organ & designing the grill to match the the church windows.
Joanne was born.
Willard Peterson decided for the Christian ministry.
Leader of Morning Watch Service for Conference Youth Institute, 600 youth.

New London: Invited to teach at Iowa Wesleyan College in addition to my church responsibilities.
Rodney was born.
Invited to move to Des Moines by Bishop Brashares and the State Committee.

36

DES MOINES AND IOWA DAYS - 1944-1953

We moved to Des Moines in October of 1944. Our salary was less than it had been in New London. The laymen of our church could not understand why anyone would move for less salary. It was a good experience for us and for them. When will we realize that money is not the only thing in life? My income had been better because of the combination of teaching and serving the church. In Des Moines we had to find a place to live because there wasn't a parsonage. Lindhorst was a layman, not a minister. The war was on and rentals were almost impossible to find. Strange that we did locate a house with lovely fireplace, oak floors, full basement, three bed rooms, two stories....and empty....located at 1647 York. We had very limited savings, and I mean limited, but enough to make a down payment for the $7,500.00 home. It proved to be a very comfortable place to live for the next ten years.

The real struggle came to me personally as I considered that great shift in my ministry. I had always thought of myself as being a pastor to a congregation....probably ending up in a county seat town in Iowa. I liked books, people and my family....and home. If I had any talents, it was developing long friendships with people and building a congregation over a period of time. Now I faced just the opposite. Touch and go.... with people and churches and congregations. Lindhorst could lead singing at the youth conferences....I could hardly carry a tune. I had proven to some extent my ability to serve a church. I might fall right on my face in this new endeavor. The struggle was one of SECURITY where I was vs. ADVENTURE to where I was going. So much depended upon me. Now we had 3 children. I had just had my 36th birthday. As I look back upon it now, it was another push from somewhere by someone to keep me from settling

down. <u>Struggle</u> <u>and</u> <u>challenge</u> has been a part of my life through the years
and I now rejoice that they were.

My first assignment was to address the Northwest Iowa Annual Conference in session at Estherville. That town is in the north-west part
of the state. During the years that followed I spoke and preached in
almost all of the churches of Iowa....big and small. I spoke to most all
of the summer camps and Institutes....including Summer Family Camp that
our family enjoyed and will remember. I developed a staff of 8 people
and established a book store at 910 tenth street. It has now become an
Abingdon-Cokesbury bookstore. Rev. and Mrs. W. M. Hubbard were very
important to my work. I brought them to my staff from their pastorate at
Clearlake. He handled the book store and Mrs. Hubbard, who was a nationally
known writer and leader of Junior age children, worked across the State.

The main thrust of my work with my staff was to enrich the work of
the local church schools of the 800 churches. This was done through
spending weekends in local communities, preaching on the meaning of
Christian education, and spending afternoons and evenings with church
school teachers. We often had weekend <u>Observation</u> <u>Schools</u>....where
actual teaching took place and teachers observed the various methods
and approaches to the task. Evaluation of these sessions always followed.

Laboratory Schools were held on a district level and extended for a
full week. Guest teachers on the regional & national level were brought
in to teach classes from Kindergarden through Junior High were held in
the mornings and evaluation sessions in the afternoon. We used many
audio-visual aids. Curriculum materials and goals were examined and in-
terpreted.

Christian education is not limited to any one age and therefore
extended to include all age groups. Therefore my responsibilities ex-

tended to the 4 Methodist Colleges in Iowa....Simpson, Morningside,
Cornell and Mt. Pleasant. I worked with their college presidents on many
projects....including faculty workshops. The presidents were Edwin E.
Voigt, (Simpson), Earl Roadman (Morningside), Russell Cole (Cornell), and
Raymond Chadwick, (Wesleyan). Iowa Wesleyan, where I had taught earlier,
granted me the honorary degree Doctor of Divinity at their commencement
in June of 1946.

Helen was a great companion...stayed at home day after day and night
after night....while I was gone. My travels took me all over the North
Central Jursidication. Rodney had problems with asthma. One night I had
just checked into the hotel at Ft. Dodge and she called me. He had to go
to the hospital. I checked out immediately and came home. And it was
here in our home that Helen and I entertained some of the greatest scholars
and leaders in our church. That group included:

    William Warren Sweet, Dallas, author and historian
    Roy L. Smith, minister, author of 40 books, noted lecturer, Chicago
    Bishop Charles W. Brashares and his wife
    John O. Gross, Director of Education for Methodism, Nashville, Tenn.
    Pastors and laymen from Iowa's largest churches
    Area Staff and Area Commission....and many others.

I remember when Dr. Sweet was eating at our table he mentioned Peabody
College in Nashville. The kids had never heard of such a place and they
giggled. Memories are rich and wonderful. One day, a Sunday, we were
ready for our prayer before dinner and Joanne asked if she could say the
prayer. Holding hands she started saying the Lord's Prayer and half way
through she forgot the rest of it. Quick as a wink Helen....joined in
and we all joined her and finished beautifully. That's what a family is
for....to help one another and support each other when we need it. That
experience has always been a cherished memory.

39

We chose Wesley Methodist for our church home. It had a long record of strong ministerial leadership and missionary outreach. We had state-wide training conferences for church institutes and camps. These groups would number 300 to 350 persons. I always arranged top notch leadership - Bishops and leaders from the National Board of Education in Nashville.

We arranged a one week trip each year to the United Nations. The group was limited to 50 lay persons. Eleanor Roosevelt met with our group one year. These seminars continued for 6 years.

I became chairman of the Iowa Council of Churches Commission on Mass Media.--radio and television. The government had put a freeze on TV station development. The only station we had in Iowa at that time was an educational station at Iowa State College in Ames, whose call letters were WOI-TV. The commission sent me to New York as a participant in a workshop, sponsored by the National Council of Churches. This was my first trip to New York, alone, and I will never forget it. I went many times afterwards, but I never took the trips lightly.

As a result of this radio and TV chairmanship, we arranged several workshops at Ames, using WOI facilities. At about this time the children said, "Dad, you can't be the head of such a group and not have TV in your own home". Well, they had a good argument, and Helen and I bought our first TV set. For once, I was glad they had talked us into it; they will tell you that they were not always so successful! From this experience I was motivated years later to introduce a college course at Southwestern. It was taught by Rachel (Van Cleve) Swomberg. The station was KARD in Wichita and they cooperated with the college on a Founder's Day program in 1960-Southwestern's 75th Anniversary. Helen Graham worked on a dramatic presentation. She found

a framed picture of the seven men who founded Southwestern in 1885. I took the picture to the TV studio, and as the program started, I was shown, then they turned the cameras to the photograph of the founders. They switched to another shot, and then to the founders. But, this time the founders were REAL. Helen had dressed 6 students and Dale Dunlap in long coats, stiff collars, etc., - the dress of the '85's. Her biggest problem was in finding men who didn't have a 'butch' haircut. She had to use wigs to resemble the style of the 80's. On the second shot, then, the watching audience was amazed to see one of the men in the photograph (they thought) reach up and scratch his head! A second man walked out in front of the committee, presented the resolution that the new college be located at Winfield, Kansas and the vote was unanimous.

At Simpson College one summer I conducted a workshop on "Religion and Public Education". It was on a statewide level and brought together people like Agnes Samuelson, who was state superintendent of Public Instruction, personnel from Iowa University and leadership of our church. This was breaking ground in a new area.

At Cornell College the following summer I conducted a workshop on "Church and State" with Dr. Warren Sweet, noted church historian as guest leader, along with others.

NORTH CENTRAL JURISDICTION

I was elected an alternate delegate to the North Central Jurisdictional conference in 1962. The family went with me to Milwaukee where the conference was held that year. I voted for Edwin E. Voigt who was assigned to the Dakota area, and I also voted for Gerald Ensley who was elected and assigned to the Iowa area. He was my new boss! I'm sure our three children remember that Milwaukee trip and the fun we had. Do you remember

watching TV in the hotel room while Dad and Mother attended conference?
"Leave the door locked and <u>do</u> <u>not</u> leave the room for <u>anything</u>. (Even
jelly beans!)" Bishop Brashares, whom we'd learned to love, was moved to
the Chicago area.

I was selected to be chairman of the Ensley Inaugural. It was a
great event that brought together ministers and lay leaders from all over
the state. We'd planned an academic procession for 10 blocks through
main street downtown (the event was at First Methodist church, the downtown church). That was the day Eisenhower's special train pulled into
Des Moines in his campaign for the presidency. We couldn't postpone our
big event, and in spite of that competition the sanctuary was filled to
capacity. Bishop Francis McConnell of Ohio was Bishop Ensley's Uncle
and Bishop Clifford Northcutt of Wisconsin were the two bishops in
attendance.

DRAKE UNIVERSITY

During these years I had the unusual experience of teaching some
courses at the Drake University School of Religion. Drake was a school
sponsored by the Christian church and has always had a fine academic
standing. I met a man there by the name of John Trevor, who was a bib-
lical scholar. Some years later our paths crossed again when he was a
resource person on a trip we took entitled "The Cradle of our Christian
Faith". It took us to Egypt, Israel, Italy & Corinth. John was in on
the discovery of the Dead Sea Scrolls near the Dead Sea, and it was a
privilege to have him in seminars on board ship. He even held extra
sessions for those of us who were interested. He is now at Claremont
School of Theology in California.

My state position in Iowa gave me unusual exposure to the North
Central Jurisdiction, and to a national audience of leaders in the state
and in other areas. I was a member of the Eisenhower "Whitehouse National

42

Youth Conference." Our delegates were to go to Washington, but we first had a meeting in the Iowa House of Representatives to prepare us for the national meeting. I was selected to make the keynote address. My theme was "On With The Dream." I used Madame Currie's discovery of radium as the opening illustration.

It was the experience of 10 years on the state, regional and national level, and my 10 years in the local pastorate that laid the foundation for my 18½ years at Southwestern College. Strange that we can see now so much clearer than we could see then the hand of God in so many ways. I was being prepared for college administration. I feel sorry for men who come out of a classroom or a medium sized church and are thrust into the awesome responsibility of college administration.

I was at Perry, Iowa, when I received a call from Raymond Dewey, trustee of Southwestern, district superintendent of the Winfield district. At this time he was interim president of the college. He was informing me that I had been elected president of the college, my alma mater, and by unanimous vote! Three weeks earlier Helen and I had met with the search committee in the Shocker Room of the Lassen Hotel in Wichita. Earlier we had been in Winfield, walked across the campus and were impressed with the friendly smiles and greetings from students we would meet. They had no idea who we were. Helen remembers Sam Wallingford asking her, "Do you think you can be the wife of a college president?" She didn't know how to reply to that one. Leave it to Sam to get to the crux of the matter! But they were a "search" committee in every sense of the word.

43

I called Helen from Perry to tell her that we'd been invited (we'd made the decision that we would go if they wanted us). Sheryl was a senior in high school, Joanne 7th grade and Rodney a fourth grader. We all knew the risk we were taking. The children were not excited about the move and Helen and I were apprehensive. That evening, Helen was going to a meeting and she knew she had to take time to talk to the children. At the close of her talk with them, they stood and formed a prayer circle. They prayed that we would all stand together and support one another, and especially support Dad, who would need an understanding family as we moved to Kansas. What a beautiful thing to do - and I really believe that our family has faithfully fulfilled that prayer through the years.

It was about midnight on New Years Eve that we crossed the Missouri border into Kansas. We were leaving Iowa after 20 years, returning to my native state. No, we were not leaving Iowa! Much of Iowa was with us. Three children were born there. Twenty years of wonderful exper-ience - more important than we realized at the time. Iowa had been really a great training for the task that I now faced.

I said to Helen that last week that we were in Des Moines that we must take some object from Iowa around which we could center our thoughts. We finally decided it should be a Grant Wood painting. Not an original - but a beautiful print. And that is exactly what we did. We purchased the print entitled "Stone City". Wood was Iowa's celebrated artist. He rose to fame in 1930 when he returned from Europe. When he stepped off the train at Cedar Rapids he saw his mother and his dentist waiting

for him. His father had died. That provided the inspiration for his painting entitled, "The American Gothic," that won first place in the Chicago Worlds Fair. He was a boyhood chum of William Shirer. Shirer became a foreign correspondent in Europe, and later India. This is all discussed in his book entitled, "The Twentieth Century Journey." They both graduated from Coe College. Grant Wood died of cancer early in his teaching career at the University of Iowa. The 'Stone City' painting hangs in our home and it is admired daily.

What would have happened if I had not gone to Iowa? One has to be away from a state for awhile before he is invited to return. I am convinced that had I returned to Kansas to start my ministry, I never would have had the opportunity to do what we did for Southwestern. How do you explain such events? We were mighty grateful for that decision in Denver in 1933. I think this is like the hand of God.

Dm. Paper.

THURS., SEPT. 13, 1945. DES

EDUCATION POST TO C. O. STROHL

The Rev. Raymond M. Shipman of Muscatine, Ia., area chairman of Christian education for the Methodist church, Wednesday announced appointment of the Rev. C. Orville Strohl as area counselor of Christian education.

Now pastor of the Methodist church at New London, Ia., the Rev. Mr. Strohl will succeed the Rev. Frank A. Lindhorst, who resigned recently to join the faculty of the College of the Pacific at Stockton, Cal.

Mr. Strohl has held pastorates at Carlisle, Madrid and New London since coming to Iowa in 1934. He was graduated from Iliff Theological seminary at Denver, Colo. He received his master's degree there and now is working on his doctorate.

This letter is from my District Superintendent, who assigned us to Carlisle in September of 1954. Twenty years later he wrote us as we were preparing to go to Southwestern College.

There is a host of letters from Iowa ministers and laymen similar to this one in my steel file. One letter from Park Anderson at Marshalltown said, "Please don't let anyone in a college set-up meddle with your humility or your down-right wholesome faith".

RAYMOND M. SHIPMAN
1221 MARSTON AVENUE
AMES, IOWA

December 1, 1953

Dear Orville:

I heard the other day of your leaving us and I have just
had the official word of it in the notice sent me by the bishop of
your transfer to the Central Kansas conference. I am very regretful
over your going, just as I was over Raoul's transfer. Two very good
friends are now being separated by a considerable distance.

However I am not surprised. I have had intimations that
offers were being made to you and so I was prepared for your going,
feeling that we could not expect to keep you permanently. It is very
interesting to observe the career of the young theological graduate
whom I assigned to Carlisle in 1934 and to see what has happened to him
since that time. I have been immensely proud of the work you have
done in your present office. You know we felt that the man who was to
follow Lindhorst should be a man of experience and yet the man who came
to that work without experience in that field has proved to be the very
man who should be there. You have grown in the work and the work has
grown greatly under you. I hope that you will have a similar experience at Southwestern. Filling your place will not be easy. I am very
glad that I do not have any responsibility in that matter. Yet there
are two assignments of which I am proud because of having had a share
in them. One is yours and the other is Sam Nichols' for I helped
send him to Collegiate church the last session when I was in the cabinet.

Pinnell told me that Southwestern is your alma mater and that
you had your first date with Helen there. I suppose you were as ig-
norant of what was to come from that as I was when I sent you to Carlisle. I'll be sorry to have her away too for though I did not see her
often it was always pleasant to meet her. I'd think she would make a
very delightful college presidents' wife, even though as yet she has
had no experience in that field. Like you in your present work she will
learn.

I remember many times when I held the last quarterly conference
for you at Carlisle on my final visit there. There was such a fine
set of reports, so different from what I had been having and so different a spirit and I finally settled back in my chair and said, " This
just doesn't seem like Carlisle." Perhaps by and by some one will be
saying, "This doesn't seem like Southwestern." I don't know anything about the situation there but I feel sure that you can bring a
fine spirit there and that the people will be glad that you came.

Perhaps I'll be able to see you before you leave. I hope so.

As ever,

PART THREE

45

PART THREE

"WHERE SELDOM IS HEARD" - KANSAS

We all left Des Moines on the night of December 31, 1953. I had
worked at the office all day finishing up my responsibilities. The furniture had been loaded during the day. We drove all night, stopping once
in awhile for a change of drivers. Once we stopped and Rodney was wide
awake, so he watched the time while we had a fifteen minute nap. There
was a full moon that night and the landscape was beautiful.

We arrived in Winfield at 8:00 a.m. on January 1, 1954, and went
to the Sonner Motel where we slept until noon. Raymond and Sylvia Dewey
took us to lunch at a nice restaurant downtown, then Orville and Raymond
went to the college office. The children ate at Curley's little hamburger
diner that day. That was their introduction to Curley's Bar-B-Que sauce!

46

Our furniture was being unloaded at the President's home, so that's
where Helen spent the afternoon. Students were all gone for the holidays.
Rod and Jody went to explore the campus and found their first tumbleweeds.
They brought one home. I reported that to Dad and Mother Burgner in my
first letter, and Dad's reply was, "They'll see enough of them in the
next few years". He just laughed and laughed. With the help of some
people from maintenance (who worked even on holiday breaks) we were soon
settled and spent the first night in our new home. That month we dedicated
our home with a special ceremony and while we were at the college dining
room for dinner several bouquets arrived. I can remember the thrill I
received at the sight. That day the family was introduced to Darwin and
Beth Wells. They'd heard about the open house, and came up with their
minister and his family. They had a baby, and Sheryl went out to the car
and sat with the child while they came in for refreshments. Years later,
Darwin told us, "Two ladies impressed me that day....Helen Strohl and
Louise Juergens". We became life-long friends.

THE PRESIDENTS OFFICE

The President's office was so empty! When I pulled open the middle
desk drawer I found a half empty bottle of aspirin and a note attached:
"Good Luck"! I did three things in my office that New Years Day that were
to serve as landmarks and reminders of my basic purpose: I hung on the
wall back of the desk the large rectangular picture entitled "Horizons".
It pictured a young man sitting at the top of a hill looking out over the
valley, pondering the tomorrows. That's what college is all about....
students searching for the meaning of life. Another picture "The Endless
Line of Splendor" pictured pioneers, marching with their covered wagons
drawn by horses. We must never forget the past and I wanted to remember
the great days of Southwestern and the sacrifices that many had made.

47

Then, I placed on my desk a copy of the Revised Standard Version of the Bible. That book represented the foundation upon which civilization is built - including a church-related college like Southwestern. These three things remained in my office for my entire tenure. They became points of interest and I discussed them often with parents, students, friends and alumni.

What a lonesome fear as I sat there. So silent in the office and throughout the building. "Miles to go before I could sleep", I thought. What I didn't know was all the skilled and dedicated help that a few of the trustees would provide. Allan Felt was Chairman of the Board of Trustees. He was willing to travel with me and did. He introduced me to Ben Christy, to the Suttons and others in Kansas. He went to Chicago with me to study the endowment proposal that the General Board of Education had made. He gave gladly and freely. What a help he was!

Sam Wallingford was a giant. Everybody in Wichita knew Sam. These men had great faith in me. Sam flew to Scott City with me to see Christy in 1954. Wallingford Hall was named for him because of his great and tremendous leadership and his large gifts. Olive Ann Beech provided her personal plane and took 5 of us out to Scott City to see Ben Christy. She was Chairman of the Endowment Committee for years and gave great leadership to it. Later we added Arthur Smith, Ph.D. in Economics and Vice President of the First National Bank in Dallas. Mrs. Beech was a "drawing card" in my work.

Others included Wm. Broadhurst, Bishop Dana Dawson, Raymond Dewey, District Superintendent and 3 local men, R. H. Pierce, Joe R. Everly, and W. W. Keith. Without the help of these and others, I never would have made it.

48

My mother had been living in Des Moines near us and her two sisters. She had been in failing health. Our move meant a move for her too. She hadn't expected to get to return to Winfield to live out her days. She spent a few days with Eugene and Billie in Kansas City til we could get settled a bit, then came on to Winfield. We found her an apartment on Maris Street.

The administration building at Southwestern had been destroyed by fire in 1950 and was 2/3 rebuilt when we came.* There was a debt of $300,000 on it....a loan made by Mr. Broadhurst's Foundation. Student enrollment was a little over 300. Faculty salaries were at an all-time low. My salary that first year was $7,400.00. It remained at that level for 3 years. The endowment was $540,000. The campus had only one dormitory, Smith Hall, built in 1923. The men's dorm was army barracks moved in from Strother Field and the Student Center was also two barracks put together. The Science Hall was new.

My first public appearance in Winfield was at First Methodist Church, where my parents, Eugene, and I had joined in 1923. Grace Raymond was on the front seat. We were dinner guests of John and Sherlah King. John and I had started Southwestern together in 1927.

Mother was well known in Winfield, having lived there for several years. Many of her friends called on her when she returned and they said, "Why did Orville become President of Southwestern? It just can't be saved. Other men have tried and failed and we don't want to see him fail". That worried Mother and she would pass the remarks on to me. To tell the truth, I was a little worried too!

* The actual date of the fire was April 16, 1950

A BULWARK NEVER FAILING

On January 16, 1954, the Executive Committee inaugurated the Washington Semester at American University. That day we also renewed our pledge to the Methodist ministers of our conference. A copy of my first letter is attached. These letters were followed up every few months. We have always loved the local church. She gave the college its life. She sent us her strongest students. She supported us with her stewardship. She welcomed me as president to her pulpits. She invited our musical groups as well as our admission counselors into her churches. The church has been, and continues to be a "Mighty Bulwark Never Failing."

After 18½ years as President I returned to the local church as an associate minister. Richard Robbins, now Superintendent of the Wichita district said to mé "Orville, I am so pleased to see you at work in a local congregation. So many men who have been in connectional work never return to the local church again. You have put your actions where you have put your words." Thank you Dick, a Southwestern graduate, for that insight.

SOUTHWESTERN COLLEGE
WINFIELD, KANSAS

OFFICE OF THE PRESIDENT

January 16, 1954

Dear Pastors:

As I write this first letter to you I have a prayer in my heart that
this may be the beginning of a warm-hearted fellowship among us, that
we shall never forget and treasure always. My ministry has always
been focused on the local church and I see no reason for changing it
now. I have never lost my interest in, nor my love for, the work of
the local parish. Therefore, I trust you will count on me as a co-
laborer with you in the interest of God's Kingdom.

I want to keep you informed about your college and these 400 fine
stalwart youth. No greater compliment could be paid Southwestern
College than the willingness and desire of parents to have their sons
and daughters enrolled as students. Ours is a sacred trust that we
shall never forget. The enclosed calendar brings to your attention
important dates for you, for your seniors, their parents and others.

I would appreciate receiving from you news of your church, parish
papers or news bulletins.

The Rev. Phillip Chastain started January 4th as Admissions Counselor.
He is in the field now. If you could use him to an advantage, write
him here at the College. Meanwhile, the names of the seniors and
juniors and also those who are attending junior college would be helpful. We are working for at least 500 students next fall. You can
help us greatly by counseling with your finest young people about
Southwestern.

We will be glad to send to any pastor the fine set of 2x2 colored slides
of the buildings on the campus. Could you use this in an evening MYF
session and call it "Southwestern Night"? If you could use talent
from the college faculty or staff or a student team, we will be glad
to cooperate with you. I am anxious to get better acquainted with
you and your laymen. I will be glad to preach or be used in any other
activity of the church's program. Our calendar is filling up fast,
however, and dates need to be scheduled several months ahead.

Blessings upon each of you and your families for this New Year of 1954.

Most sincerely,

C. Orville Strohl
President

COS:rb

49

INTERNATIONAL EDUCATION

I had my first executive committee of the board of trustees on Jan. 16, 1954. I recommended that Southwestern establish the <u>Washington Semester</u> at American University, Washington, D.C. They did and the first student to go in the fall semester of the following year was Wanda Bradbury. She wrote a letter saying, "Did you see my picture in the Washington Post? I was over on Capitol Hill when Secretary of State, John Foster Dulles, returned from India. I was at his press conference and happened to be in a picture taken of him". I was able to get a copy of the picture for our college publication. This was the beginning of an ever-broadening program in International Education for Southwestern students and faculty. A few years later, a group of five college presidents were spending a weekend together. It was out of that meeting that we said, "If we can have a program at American University, why not a United Nations Semester at Drew University?". Drew was only a few miles from New York City and United Nations Headquarters. We wrote to the President of Drew University and laid our plan before him. He cooperated without delay, saying "Why didn't I see that opportunity? I would let some Presidents from mid-western colleges think of it!".

Out of these experiences came others.* The Pacific Area Seminar at the East-West Center in Honolulu. Helen and I were attending a seminar there and saw the chance for our students to broaden their horizons. And the program at the University of Graz, Austria, was tremendous. It was too expensive for many of our students who wanted to go.

Before long a group of Methodist Colleges was organized into "The Association of Colleges and Universities for International and Intercultural Studies". I was a charter member of that group and served on the Board of

* Exchange with Spellman College started in 1975.

50

Directors until 1972. A certificate of Appreciation, signed by Richard Bender, hangs on the wall of my study. Two members of our faculty spent a Summer in study in Bierut, Lebanon and have been so concerned and depressed at the recent events there; the destruction and loss of life.*

In 1960, Dr. John O. Gross who was executive director of the Board of Higher Education planned a 6-week trip to Europe for 12 Methodist College Presidents. Dr. Ralph Decker was the leader. I was invited to go, and what a privilege it was. Highlights were to see what was being done in Russia and other communist countries in the name of education. It was certainly different than our concept. This trip was in Oct. and Nov. of 1960.

In the Summer of 1960 two of our students (Juniors) had gone to Russia. That trip was sponsored by the Y.M.C.A. They visited youth camps and spent their time with them. Before they left Russia they invited the youth to come and visit our country. A group of them began to make plans and applied for their visas. After considerable time had elapsed, their visas were not granted. The press in Russia said they were denied visas by the U.S. State Department. Our students, James Schultz and Larry Montgomery, came to me in September criticizing our State Department and were adament in their reaction. I was not able to answer their questions, but told them I would do what I could to find the answer for them while I was in Russia. While in Moscow I went to the American Embassy and told them the story. Here is their answer: "The Russian government 'sat' on the requests for visas until the day before the trip was to be made. Then they released them to the United States. There was no way a visa could be processed in 24 hours! Their story was only

* This story was written in 1982, at the time of the invasion.

partly true. The visas did not reach our State Department in time!
Jim and Larry had their eyes opened. These two students were expelled
from the Soviet Union because Jim gave a small copy of the gospel of John
to a Russian youth. The news hit all the newspapers and was made to be
a 'big deal'.

In the trip with the college presidents we went to Helsinki, Lenin-
grad, Moscow, Kiev, Prague, East Germany, Berlin, Rome, Paris, London
Bath and Bristol. Two of our men were black. This was a very wise
choice because no one stands higher in Russia than educators. And for two
black men to be college administrators in the United States was exhibit
one. We did something to refute their propoganda that the U.S. mistreated blacks.

The basic purpose of the trip was to study education, on all levels,
in Soviet dominated countries. Appointments had been made for us ahead
of time with the Rectors (Russia's name for Presidents) and their staffs.
In this way we wasted no time and went to work immediately. Six weeks is
not much time, but long enough under those conditions to get a lot done
and develop some life long viewpoints. We were in Red Square, rode the
beautiful subways in Moscow, were in the Kremlin and visited the American
Embassies of each country we visited. What a contrast to see their educational program against ours.

As we flew over the Statue Of Liberty coming into New York, we
recalled the words, "Give me your poor.......". We were home!

Before we parted to return to our own campuses we made a covenant
to bring as many African students to our campus as possible. Russia

was saying Blacks should not go to the United States because they would
be mistreated. The Soviet Union was in the process of establishing
a new university for African students called "Free University". But,
instead of being free, the students were completely segregated, dominated
and controlled. We brought several students from Africa each year
following this exchange.

BUILDERS AROUND THE WORLD

In a President's Advisory Committee meeting one day we were talking
about Southwestern's outreach around the world. A few months earlier
I had been in Washington, D.C. I went to see Ambassador Loy Henderson,
who was one of 'the greats' in the State Department. He had been an
ambassador to Iran, and other nations. He had just retired from active
duty. As I walked into his home I passed by his ambassador's flag there
in the front hall. I admired it. He said, "What am I going to do with
that flag?" When I discovered that he was serious I made a suggestion.
"Look Mr. Henderson, give that flag to your Alma Mater and we will make
it the 'core' around which our international program revolves. He con-
sented to send it to us. And so, in the advisory committee meeting I
reported this conversation and announced the gift. It was Tom Wallraben-
stein who suggested the theme "Builders Around The World". On
Founders Day of that year, March 2, 1964, we invited Ben Hibbs, who
was corresponding editor for the Readers Digest, as our speaker.
Ambassador Henderson was present. Dr. Louis Sudler from Chicago sang,
"All Peoples Of The Earth, Share But One Common Birth". Flags of 21
countries, from which students had come, were flying. Special flag poles
were placed in the cement around the driveway south of Christy. We
secured the flags through the United Nations.

THE DANIEL EBONG STORY - AN EXAMPLE!

WRITTEN IN FEBRUARY, 1974

Here is an unusual story of a remarkable family linking Nigeria,
Africa and Southwestern College together in Christian love.

In July of 1958 a young man from Nigeria, by the name of Daniel Ebong,
spoke at the Methodist camp at Horizon. On his way back to Kansas City he
stopped at the President's office at Southwestern College to ask if he could
enroll in September. He said, "I have no money, but I am willing to work.
For this past year I have been enrolled in a college that is not accredited,
and my Government will not recognize a degree from an unaccredited college.
What little money I had left after getting to the States has been spent."

The fiscal year of the College had ended on June 30. I had the reports
on my desk. We were $2,000 in the red regarding our scholarships for foreign
students. I was caught between a rock and a hard place. Having no idea
where I could get that much money, I told Mr. Ebong that we just couldn't
accept him. But, I did make arrangements for him to eat lunch at the College.

I went home for lunch and found Helen hard at work with books and the
typewriter. No lunch was in sight. I said, "Helen, what are you doing?"
"I'm working on a missionary lesson for the women at Grace Methodist Church
tomorrow afternoon," she replied. That gave me time to think! Was I going
to let Helen talk about missions .... we are long on verbalizing our faith...
and turn down an actual opportunity to educate a student from another country
in a Methodist college? Surely there would be a way open.

We prayed as we started our lunch together, and before I had finished I called the dining hall and left word for Mr. Ebong to return to my office. When he came in, I told him that I had changed my mind, and that if he would get his papers ready, he could enroll. This he did.

Mr. Ebong was one of our students for three years, graduating in 1961. During that time, he won all of our hearts. He traveled with me to visit many churches and represented the college in many civic and educational groups. He kept telling me about his wife and four children back in Nigeria.

A few weeks before Commencement some of our students came to my office with a very attractive "Friendship Scroll" made by the art department. They wanted me to sign it along with them. They said, "We wanted you to place the college seal upon it, but your secretary says that the seal is used for official documents only. We understand." I replied, "If this friendship scroll is not official, then I don't know what is. I will be glad to inscribe it with the college seal."

The next evening, the same group of students invited Helen and me to attend a small dinner party for Daniel at the student center. The scroll was presented, along with a special copy of the Moundbuilder, the college yearbook, and the students told Daniel what he had meant to them and to the campus. They also had learned his native song, and we sang it together with feeling. The evening closed with a prayer circle with a number of prayers. I shall never forget the inspiration of those moments.

From June, 1967, through January, 1971, the Biafra war and revolution took place in Nigeria. Daniel and his family were caught in that conflict and he was separated from his family from March, 1968, to January, 1970. During that time, they did not know if he was alive or dead.

It was at that time that I heard from Mr. Ebong's son, Imeh. He said, "I pray that I may be able to attend my father's Alma Mater." In September, 1970, he was enrolled, and one year later his sister, Grace, also enrolled.

These two young people are the salt of the earth. They, too, have gone into many churches, clubs and educational groups telling the story of their family and their country. This family is the product of the missionary outreach of the church. They are all outstanding Christian people. Both Imeh and Grace are working many hours at the Winfield State Hospital and Training Center, and, earlier, at William Newton Memorial Hospital.

On Sunday, May 19, both of these young people will be graduating..... from their father's Alma Mater. They are looking forward to graduate school here in the States before returning to Nigeria.

Now, the pay-off! A few of us have a dream of bringing their parents to Winfield for Commencement. The cost is greatly reduced if they come on what is known as the International Excursion Fare. They must stay in the States at least 14 days and not more than 21 days. This would permit them to be at the Annual Conference of our church and be available for a limited number of appearances. The air fare is $1,800 for both of them both ways. We should add another $100 for other expenses. Of the $1,900 needed, we already have $1,300.

This is Missions at its best! This is the love of Christ binding two peoples together. I am glad Helen was working on a missionary lesson. She had no idea how effective it was going to be.

Later - Mr. Ebong could not leave his work in Nigeria because he was responsible for the program in Elementary Education in his country, which was being inaugurated that year. Mrs. Ebong, who had never been to the States, did come. The following is a description of the sixteen days she was here.

Grace and Imeh went to the Wichita airport with us on May 17, 1974.
It had been four years since Imeh had seen his mother and three years for
Grace. What an experience! The T.W.A. 707 taxied into position only forty
minutes late from Nigeria. NOW WE KNOW, ALL OVER AGAIN, THAT MOTHER MEANS THE
SAME TO HER CHILDREN ALL OVER THE WORLD. To see these three reunited after
so long is something we shall never forget. Finally, that attractive lady of
forty-three years of age turned to Helen and me and said in such a soft and
sincere voice ..... "I am grateful, I am grateful"....

On Saturday night we attended the Alumni Dinner at the College. They
were introduced by the president of the Alumni Association. Many friends
came by our table to greet them.

On Sunday morning we presented them and Rev. Ward Williams, an American
missionary from Zaire, whose son Mark also graduated from Southwestern this
year, to 75 adults in a church school class. After a brief fellowship, we
went to the College Baccalaureate and sat together.

At noon, 38 people were gathered for a luncheon in Pound's Lounge. These
were the people who had helped Mrs. Ebong to make the trip. We were so sorry that
some of you couldn't be present. Mrs. Ebong's brother and his family from St.
Louis joined us. It was a great and moving experience to have each person
share their love and experience with the Ebong family.

That evening at the Commencement (out-of-doors) the flags of all the nations
from which Southwestern graduates have come formed the background for the platform. The 7-year-old nephew from St. Louis saw the Nigerian flag floating in
the breeze. He watched it for a while and then, looking up at his mother, said,
"See, Mother, the Nigerian flag flies best".

President Ruthenberg had asked me to present the diplomas to both Grace and Imeh, which I was glad to do. When they walked across the platform, Mrs. Ebong, her brother and her new American friends stood in recognition. It was a proud moment for her.

The family appeared in both morning worship services at First Church, and the following Sunday at Trinity United Methodist. They had 45 minutes on K.N.I.C. Radio in Winfield. They attended the Kansas West Annual Conference in Salina. When I presented them, the Conference greeted them with an applause, and Bishop Dixon came to shake hands with them in person. Imeh was greatly impressed by the ordination service.

Friends from everywhere swarmed around them for the full day and a half that they were in Salina. On Friday we took them to the Eisenhower Center in Abilene. President Eisenhower was in office when Daniel was in college in Winfield. Of course, Mrs. Ebong remembered his activities in Europe.

Mrs. R. B. White arranged a visit to the Binney and Smith Crayola Factory in Winfield. They were in many homes. Mrs. Eckel had a beautiful luncheon in Douglass. They saw Mrs. Harris' ranch in Oklahoma. They had a reception at Grace United Methodist Church one evening, and met many new friends at a bar-b-que in the Strohl's backyard. They visited the zoo in Wichita, and Mrs. Ebong saw for the first time a lion and an elephant. (How did we get Kansas confused with Africa?)

On Sunday night, June 2, we had a farewell fellowship for them at First United Methodist Church. Grace spoke about Nigeria. Her mother talked about her 24 years of teaching experience, and Imeh talked about the power and significance of the Church of Jesus Christ. It all ended when 160 people formed a great fellowship circle around the sanctuary and sang and prayed.

The CHURCH welcomed her to the States and the CHURCH sent her on her way as she returned to her husband, Daniel, and four children.

Grace and Imeh both will be in graduate school at Wichita State next fall. She is working for her M.A. in accounting and Imeh is working on his M.S. in physics.

There is something very significant about this link of Christian fellowship that you and I have formed with Nigeria through this unusual family. To me it is nothing less than the hand of God at work in our midst. Mrs. Ebong's father took her to school on his bicycle three miles when she was a very little girl and at a time when girls were not considered worth educating. Remember also how I almost turned Daniel down in July of 1958.

The new Nigerian Head of State, General Gowin, is a Christian, and only 39 years of age. Nigeria is our second largest supplier of oil.

We have left in our account about $1,000.00. At First Church here in Winfield we are willing to start an Ebong scholarship fund to help these two young people to meet the expenses of their graduate work. Incidentally, Imeh says he wants to get his Ph.D. in Physics. Imagine that! He came to Southwestern when his father was a prisoner in the civil war of Nigeria back in 1969. Now he dreams of a Ph.D. in America! *The Church and her college has brought him on his way.

Helen and I have never had an experience quite like this one before, even though we have worked with young people for many years.

* In December of 1981 he was granted the Ph.D. degree in Nuclear Physics from Arizona State. Helen and I wanted to be there for that high moment but we could not go. I told him the summer before to call us collect before he left the States for Lagos, Nigeria. One morning in December, about 8:00 a.m., the telephone rang and Helen answered. The operator said, "Ebong calling from New York for Dr. Strohl." Helen thought the operator said "Avon", and said so as she handed me the phone. It was Imeh Ebong calling to say, "Thank you for all your help and goodbye. I am leaving for the capitol of my country, Lagos, where I will be teaching at the University."

This is the most dramatic example of International Education because it involves a whole family and a span of over twenty years. But there were many others..... such as Anita Maldonado from Mexico, whose final destination became the United Christian Hospital in Lahore, Pakistan. Or, Christine Wolfe from Mexico City. Or, Billie Day from Littleton, Colorado, who became an administrator under Sargeant Shriver and served in Africa with the Peace Corps. It was Billie who called from Freetown, Africa, about Raymond George, who came, graduated and returned.

"Builders Around The World" is a reality!

THE INAUGURAL   1955 - MARCH

It was my request that the Inaugural be delayed a year so that I could
get my feet on the ground. After all, the ceremony would not make or break
our administration. So, Founders Day of 1955 became the accepted time (March 11-15).

As happens with most such affairs, we had a number of speakers from afar.
Most special was Dr. Harold Bosley, minister of the First Methodist Church
in Evanston; Bishop Edwin E. Voigt, from the Dakota area, who had been President
of Simpson College in Iowa; U.S. Congressman Clifford Hope, from District 1
(Western Kansas) and Herbert Clutter from Holcomb, Kansas. (It was the
Clutter family who was later slaughtered by two ex-convicts, when Beverly,
their daughter, was a student at Southwestern College. The news of this
tragic event came by telephone, while all of us, including Beverly, were at
Grace Methodist Church. The rose window in the New United Methodist Church
in Garden City was made possible by the students and faculty of the college.
This event came to national prominence when the book entitled. "In Cold Blood"
was written by Mr. Truman Capote.

My address entitled, "Identification Please" was an effort to set out
in simple language the reasons for Southwestern's existence.* From the
beginning, I tried to highlight the Reasons - and kept placing emphasis upon
the importance of teamwork among all of those who had any interest at all in
our future. I requested the privilege of writing the charge and The Act Of
Dedication. I knew that I could not pull out of the quagmire by myself.
It would take all of us, Trustees, faculty, students, alumni, ministers and
friends of the college, pulling together with God if the job was to be done.
These were the groups who responded to Bishop Dana Dawson's charge as they
stood to be identified. The Richardson Auditorium was completely full!!
* A copy of which is included on following pages.

THE ACT OF DEDICATION

BISHOP DANA DAWSON, D.D., LL.D., LITT.D.
The Kansas Area of the Methodist Church

THE BISHOP: C. Orville Strohl, you have been elected by the Trustees of Southwestern College and appointed by the Methodist Church, as President of this Christian Institution —a college known for its compelling Christian challenge to young life, for its broad liberal principles of education, and for its world-wide ministry of service to humanity. Take courage in these ancient words, "Have I not commanded thee; be strong and of good courage; be not affrighted, neither be thou dismayed, for the Lord thy God is with thee withersoever thou goest."

THE PRESIDENT: I will so do, the Lord being my helper.

THE BISHOP: Your task will demand the best in culture, the finest in scholarship, the highest in wisdom, that the torchlight of truth may be kept burning with increasing brightness. Therefore, thou shalt love the Lord thy God with all thy mind.

THE PRESIDENT: I will so do, the Lord being my helper.

THE BISHOP: As an administrator you will need to be courageous but charitable, firm but forgiving, fearless but fair, progressive but patient, uncompromising but cooperative, remembering "Love worketh no ill to his neighbor, therefore, love is the fulfillment of the law."

THE PRESIDENT: I will so do, the Lord being my helper.

THE BISHOP: As President of this College, your shadow of influence will fall across the paths of many people; faculty and students, ministers, members of the Church, and many others. Pray that your shadow, like that of Peter, may bring much health, healing and harmony to these who esteem you and imitate you, as you are an imitator of Christ.

THE PRESIDENT: I will so do, the Lord being my helper.

THE BISHOP: As Trustees of this College you are called to add to this dedication of your President your consecrated vision, judgment, energies, and support to the end that Southwestern shall enjoy a fruitful and stable future.

THE TRUSTEES: We will so do, the Lord being our helper. *(Trustees remain standing.)*

THE BISHOP: You are the teachers who, devoted to the service of youth, give character and life to this College. It is your part to complement a dedicated administration with dedicated scholarship, stimulating teaching, and Christian influence as together you undergird a Christian Community of Learning on this campus.

THE FACULTY: We will so do, the Lord being our helper. *(Faculty remain standing.)*

THE BISHOP: Students are the reason for the existence of Southwestern College. You are here to learn from the past and prepare for the future. It is for you to devote yourselves to the pursuit of the high ideals of scholarship and character which this College holds before you, adding your best to that of the Faculty and Administration.

THE STUDENTS: We will so do, the Lord being our helper. *(Students remain standing.)*

THE BISHOP: A College is known by the character of its graduates. It is also dependent upon them. As Southwestern College ministered faithfully and well to you and your needs in preparing you for life, so now as Alumni it is your privilege and responsibility to loyally support your Alma Mater as it ministers to your children and children's children.

THE ALUMNI: We will so do, the Lord being our helper. *(Alumni remain standing.)*

THE BISHOP: Southwestern College is the Church in higher education on this campus. It depends on the Church and in turn feeds new life into the Church. Ministers and congregations, with their prayers, their youth, and their tithes, can insure a glorious tomorrow for this College and our Church.

THE MINISTERS: We will so do, the Lord being our helper. *(Ministers remain standing.)*

THE BISHOP: This College lives by the generous loyalty of its friends. Only as those who have faith in the unique contribution of Christian higher education support it by their encouragement and their gifts will the imprint of Christianity be found on the life and culture of our country.

THE FRIENDS OF THE COLLEGE: We will so do, the Lord being our helper. *(Friends of the College will remain standing.)*

THE BISHOP: The fulfillment of the divine destiny of Southwestern College depends upon all of you—President, Trustees, Faculty, Students, Alumni, Ministers of the Conference, the Church, and Friends of the College—working together for the Glory of God.

ALL: We will so do, the Lord being our helper. *(Remain standing until after the Hymn.)*

THE INVESTITURE

In dozens of ways I hammered again and again on the basic philosophy of Southwestern. I remembered from Iowa days that I had to be "Red Hot" about my task, because the people I worked with were "Luke Warm", and the general public were "Ice Cold". This statement appeared in my inaugural brochure.

Southwestern College Makes Creative Contribution To Our Christian Culture

Higher education under private non-tax supported auspices has a genuine place in our culture and seeks to preserve its dynamic character. The church-related college, privately supported and controlled, represents a philosophy of Western Civilization that is indispensable to our way of life. Free and private education is an expression of the character of democracy. Out of that fertile soil has grown our rich heritage and the creative and unparalleled leadership of our century. Because of that, America stands in a position of world leadership.

Free and private education is in line with a historic trend stemming from the Middle Ages, the Renaissance and the Reformation. The world owes much to the concern of the Christian church for learning. It has treasured the mainsprings of freedom, of individual integrity and a desire to provide opportunity to speak and to develop convictions.

For seventy years Southwestern has had her place in this great educational movement. Here teachers have taught, prayers have been said, youth have learned and been inspired. Generations of them have marched from this campus into all parts of the world blazing new trails.

All of this has been made possible by the generosity, the sacrificial spirit, the deep and profound consecration of men and women who gave themselves in the interest of youth.

Therefore, Seventy years of glorious achievement look down upon us. Surely all of us are moved to link hands with our forefathers as we seek to enter into their labors and build here a Southwestern that shall serve our day and decade.

Southwestern reaches out to gather unto herself all those who share in this conviction. She challenges us to respond to her call. Let us arise and make her great.

C. Orville Strohl
President

Inaugural Convocation
SOUTHWESTERN COLLEGE
Winfield, Kansas

Clarence Orville Strohl, B. A., Th. M., D. D.
Thirteenth President

MARCH 11-15, 1955

Southwestern's Program in Christian Higher Education is--

"Vast in Scope—
Honorable in Intent—
Genuine in Motive"—

"With Goals that are Ambitious
Enough to be a Real Challenge
But Realistic Enough
to be Attainable"

"Old Enough to be Proven—
Strong Enough to be Challenging—
Young Enough to be Contemporary"

A college is more than a place; it is an idea and an attitude. Few men have understood its role as clearly, or described it as well as Alfred North Whitehead:

"The justification for a college is that it preserves the connection between knowledge and the zest of life, by uniting the young and the old in the imaginative consideration of learning — This atmosphere of excitement, arising from imaginative consideration, transforms knowledge. A fact is no longer a bare fact; it is invested with all its possibilities. It is no longer a burden on the memory; it is energizing as the poet of our dreams, and as the architect of our purposes."

the southwesterner

of Southwestern College in Kansas

Volume 15   Number 3   8/78

FRIDAY, SEPT. 16, 1893 No. 4

ARTHUR COVEY
© 1953
© 1953 ARTHUR COVEY

THE SOUTHWESTERNER

Published quarterly at Southwestern College, 100
North College, Winfield, Kansas. Second-class postage
paid at Winfield, Kansas 67156. Howard H. Stephens,
Editor

DR & MRS C ORVILLE STROHL
1709 MOUND
WINFIELD, KS 67156

'31 X 32

CHEROKEE STRIP

The Cherokee Strip run was made 85 years ago
this year. This pencil sketch was made 25 years
ago by Southwestern alumnus Arthur Covey.
The Covey Collection is on permanent display
on the campus and includes works in various
media: pencil, charcoal, pastel, oil, and metal.

OPENING OF THE CHEROKEE STRIP TO SETTLE...

53

THE BUILDING PROGRAM BEGINS

When we arrived in Winfield in January of 1954, my assistant was
Wendell Williams. His home had been Oxford, and that's where Mr. Broadhurst
started, so there was a long acqaintance. Wendell told him about the new
president at Southwestern. With that introduction, I called on Mr.
Broadhurst and told him I needed a 'spark' to set the new program into
action; I needed a 'shot' to get the race underway. Richardson Administration Building had burned on April 16, 1950, and had been partially
rebuilt. In February, Bill said he would give us $300,000 for a new mens
dormitory. Our facility for men at that time was re-converted barracks
from Strother Field. So, it was needed! Bill had two daughters and had
always wanted a son, so he preferred a men's dormitory. It was to house
ninety-six men, and would include lounges, study rooms, laundry facilities,
and a recreational room. His architect, Millard Buck of Bartlesville,
had been on campus and suggested to him that the building be built on the
corner of Warren and McCabe streets. I said to Bill, " Look, as much as
we appreciate and need this new dormitory, no trustee can or should decide
on his own where a building is going to be built. Any trustee could build
a "tool shed" anywhere if that policy existed. That position took courage
for a new president. So, the building and grounds committee had several
meetings, for this was a touchy subject. The decision was made that it
should be built where the old home for the president was then located,
on the corner of Warren and College Avenue. That was the beginning of the
so-called "residential campus", and the new facility would be at the entrance
to the campus where it could be seen and admired by everyone. This was
agreeable to the donor, and proved to be a wise decision.(See description
and Master Plan)

Master Plan
Southwestern College Campus
Winfield, Kansas

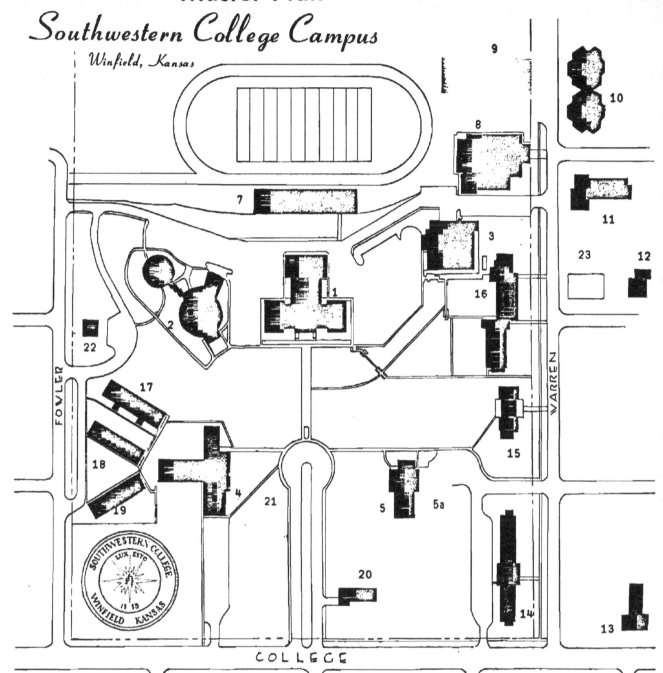

ADMINISTRATION, ACADEMIC, ATHLETIC

1. Christy Administration Building
   Richardson Auditorium
2. Darbeth Fine Arts Center
   Messenger Recital Hall
3. Roy L. Smith Student Center
4. Mossman Science Hall
5. Memorial Library Addition
5a. Frank A. White
6. Monypeny Track
7. Sonner Stadium
8. Stewart Field House
9. Site of Women's Physical Education
   Building and Swimming Pool
10. Reid Hall

RESIDENCE HALLS AND APARTMENTS

11. Sutton Hall
12. Fisher Hall
13. Holland Hall
14. Broadhurst Hall
15. Smith Hall
16. Wallingford Hall
17. Shriwise Apartments
18. Student Apartments—B Unit
19. Student Apartments—C Unit
20. The President's Residence
21. The Mound
22. Office and Classrooms
23. Tennis Courts

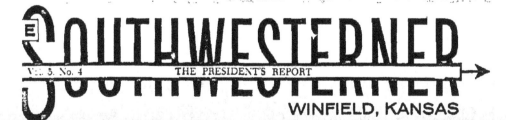

54

In early March, 1954, we observed Founder's Day. That morning in convocation I presented Mr. Broadhurst an honorary degree (also one to Olive Ann Beech) and that noon we had the luncheon in the dining room at First Methodist Church. The Broadhurst family was present, with Mr. Buck, the architect who had drawings of the new building. Dr. Myron Wicke was present, representing the national Board of Education, Nashville, Tenn. It was a great day and started us on our way in grand style - that lasted for 18½ years!

The old home for the President was moved to the north side of the campus (it didn't matter that we'd put new curtains and drapes at all the windows in that big two-story building). The trustees purchased a small but comfortable residence at 1414 E. 4th Street and we moved to that. It was the home which Dean LeRoy Allen had owned. He had been a great dean at Southwestern for a long time.

Broadhurst Hall was dedicated in Sept. 1954. It was occupied by students that school year 1954-55. It was the talk of the town! All the furnishings were provided by the Broadhurst Foundation. Some members of Faculty Dames spent many hours sewing on name tapes for sheets, blankets, and towels. These were also furnished by Mr. Broadhurst.

Residential Campus - Its Purpose and Plan

All intelligent activity must have a basic purpose and plan for its fullfillment. The purpose of Southwestern was stated in the first brochure that was published in 1955. It is stated elsewhere but let me state it again:

> "The purpose of Southwestern College is to become a residential campus, which will become a spot of beauty and a place of culture where quality education is imparted from the Christian point of view."

55

What is a residential campus? Why is it important? Why is beauty and culture a part of it?

There is a world of difference between the so called "Day School" and a campus which becomes the home for students. A day school is limited to class attendance. But the richest education involves the whole student and takes place on a campus where students live and work and play, discuss and ponder and think and worship and sometimes struggle and share in the growing-up process. A residential campus becomes a community where education goes on 24 hours a day. There are many life long decisions made in the dorms, in student organizations, in small groups of friends, in informal associations with faculty and administration. Here is an illustration. One day a couple of students came by my office to see me. They said, "We have only one reason for being here and that is to invite you to have a coke with us at the student center. We got to thinking that probably all those who come to your office make some request or have a problem. We just wanted to become better acquainted". That was very unusual but it represents the idea of a residential campus where all of us are available. Adults need students as well as students needing adults.

The plan of the campus that follows was thought through very carefully. The residential part of the campus was laid out around Warren Street. The food service was near at hand as well as the snack bar and recreational facilities....including swiming pool. The President's home became an integral part of the residential area. (Note: one morning at 7:45 two seniors came to our kitchen door on their way to class. The night before they had become engaged and Shirley was now wearing a diamond.* They wanted us to know about it....and shared that joy with us as the

* Shirley Holt and Wendell Nixon.

first ones of the college community. They now live in Colorado.) The
library is easily reached at night or in bad weather. The Shriwise Apartments, which were originally intended for married students, was placed on
the north side of the campus for more privacy but still were a part of the
college community.

A Spot of Beauty: Education is absorbed as well as learned. In 1885
the campus was placed on a hill to provide a horizon....out over the Walnut
Valley. So we engaged Mr. and Mrs. Glenn Bartlett of Belle Plaine to spend
some time studying the campus plan. Upon their recommendations we planted
trees and shrubs and did landscaping costing a total of $18,000.00 dollars.
The old spirea that stood on either side of the "77" steps was replaced
with spreaders and small junipers. The trees were Sunburst Locust, Purple
Plum, White Birch, Ball Cypress, Sugar Maple, Red Oak, Burning Bush and
many others. What could be more fitting than a campus in the Fall of the
year becoming a blaze of color and in the Spring those trees budding and
leafing out?

A Place of Culture: Music and art, recitals and concerts and a host
of other cultural events brings a student community to life. A singing
campus is a happy campus. Students and faculty need to be able to see
and feel and hear life's creative expressions. The lectureships brought
to the campus some of the finest minds and personalities to be found in
America. Such people as Ralph W. Sockman from New York, Eleanor Roosevelt
from the United Nations, Bishop G. Bromley Oxnam of Washington D.C., Dr.
Harold Bosley from Evanston, Dean Howard Thurman from the campus of Boston
University. (These lectures were later published in a book entitled
"Disciplines of the Spirit" Harper and Row), Dr. Gerald Kennedy from
California and others. The Covey Art Collection, discussed elsewhere, also
created an atmosphere of culture.

57

Early in our administration Helen and I started having formal dinners at our home for division chairmen and their spouses. This led to formal dinners for all faculty and administrative personnel and their spouses. These were held in the large dining hall. The printed invitations were sent to all which usually numbered ninety plus. Decorations consisted of cut flowers, a rose bud at each plate, and special violin music during the dinner. It was not required but most people, both men and women, wore formal clothes. Following dinner Helen served coffee and used her demitasse cups which had been purchased from all over the country, including Europe. While we do not have a record of the years that these dinners were served, we believe it was eight. Needless to say it was a tiresome job to get them ready but they have had a lasting influence on the faculty. These affairs were always in the Spring and I would announce any promotions in rank, those leaving our campus and other items of interest. These social events were a part of the cultural life of the college in keeping with our stated purpose. I share some correspondence below:

> Dear Helen:
> From Old Quebec I bring you this bit of china and hope your collection will continue to grow. Your graciousness as a hostess is a keen reality. (Aug. 1964) R.M.G.

> Dear Mrs. Strohl:
> Your "Faculty Dinner" was truly a delightful affair for which thank you seems all to inadequate. It was an evening to savor for a long time to come. There were so many unusual features that to mention one and not another would be an unintentional omission. Please extend our appreciation to Dr. Strohl also.
> Sincerely,
> Leta R.

> Dear Dr. and Mrs. Strohl:
> May Day, 1964, will always be remembered as the day of the beautiful dinner. Everything was perfect from gleaming silver and crystal to the lovely decorations and the gracious host and hostess. It all reminded us again of how much we enjoy the associations we have found here at Southwestern. Thank you so much for an inspiring as well as an entertaining evening.
> Sincerely,
> H. W.   May 12, 1963

58

Dear Dr. and Mrs. Strohl:

Roland and I wish you and Dr. Strohl to know how very much we enjoyed your hospitality on Friday evening. Certainly the occassion was one of dignity and elegance.

Yours sincerely,

M. H.   May 2, 1964

Dear Friends:

Your President's dinner, given last Saturday evening, was memorable. I don't know when I've had such a fine social experience. Your every detail was great. The beef was delicious, the dessert was exciting and good, the coffee was so right and best of all, there was congenial and lively visiting. I had a wonderful time. Please accept my thanks again.

Ever,

R. G.   May 11, 1967

<u>Education imparted from the Christian point of view</u>: We never did encourage the faculty to forsake truth and research. On a campus like this one, students need to be given the choice to <u>see</u> and <u>understand</u> truth from a Christian point of reference. It's always an option.... but it takes a skilled faculty to see both sides of a question.*

THE CAMPUS DREAM UNFOLDS

Meanwhile, Ted Mason, architect of Wichita, drew plans for the new home for presidents at a very nominal fee. Julius Powell, a contractor from Winfield, was employed to construct the home on a cost plus 10% basis. I raised all the money for it, day by day, month by month. It was modeled after the home of Mr. and Mrs. Charles English of Mulvane, and Helen and I worked on arrangements of rooms, for we planned to entertain a lot! The big question was, should we air condition? We were indebted to Arlon

* Much more should and could be said.

59

Ebright, then on the board, who insisted that it should be. Sam Wallingford, Mrs. Beech, Mrs. Fisher and many others really assisted in the financing.
Mr. Sims of Rock gave me a $12,000 annuity which was to pay for the living
room. It is 30 by 14 feet. I had told him how important that room would be
for we were going to entertain students, visit with them, and guide them as
far as we could. The day I talked to him about it, he turned me down.

The next morning, Harley Coffey of the State Bank called me and said,
"President Strohl, there is a man here who wants to talk to you". It was
Sims. He said, "I'll be right up to see you". When he arrived he said,
"I couldn't sleep last night thinking about what you said. I want students
to acquire a Christain faith while they are getting their education. So,
here is a check for $12,000 as an annuity". The home and furnishings cost
$40,000. The dedication of the ranch-style residence was in the fall of
1955. We moved in July, and our first luncheon guests were a group of men
who had met Ben Christy in Wichita and brought him to the campus. It was
Sam Wallingford & Emil Holgerson. Wally Keith, Joe Everly, and Dick Pierce
from Winfield joined us. A few days before Helen had caught a finger in
the garage doors, and was a bit incapacitated in the kitchen. Pauline Martin
catered the luncheon and Lucile Smith, wife of our business manager, (and a
good friend) helped with the serving. I remember that Sam Wallingford raved
about the lemon pie! We had two open house receptions for townspeople and
anyone interested. Mrs. Fisher was co-hostess for one, and Olive Ann Beech
for the other. I remember Olive Ann was nervous, and probably rightly so,
about Helen's ability and when she saw the first guests coming up the walk
she said, "Is everything ready in the kitchen?"

60

I first met Ben Christy in 1954, and I talked to him about our financial needs. I saw him often and he had a habit of pulling out a $5,000 check each time. Usually he would say, "Mr. President, I know you need money and I want to help" - or - "I just read one of your bulletins and I see you are trying to keep the bills paid. Maybe this will help." Generous! Yes, in a way - but it was also a way to keep me from asking for a larger amount of money which he was very able to give. So, I planned carefully with Rev. Sam Keller of the Methodist Church in Scott City for a luncheon. I said, "Sam, do you have some ladies who 'see nothing', 'hear nothing' and 'say nothing' - and who can cook? "Sure," he said. Then I told him I would be calling him and requesting a luncheon. I knew it had to be a private affair, for important matters of this kind must not be public. That would have ruined it.

So, on this special day, Olive Ann Beech furnished her plane, and she, Sam Wallingford, Emil Holgerson, Rodney and I flew to Scott City. There we met Irene Zane, manager of Sunnyslope Farm, the trainer of that famous horse, Lemon Drop Kid. We picked up Allen Felt, who was in Scott City at the time, and drove out to Sunnyslope for a 'look see'. At noon, when we stopped at the church, Mr. Christy was there to meet us. We were ready! Again, it was a great experience. Ben handed me a check for $5,000. after we'd had our first course, salad. The committee knew he would do that. We talked about the college, showed him a Moundbuilder (yearbook) and other pictures, and then I said, "Mr. Christy, we want you to do something for Southwestern that is comparable to your interest in youth, and your financial ability". (He was worth 10 million dollars)

"What do you have in mind?" he asked. I replied, " A half million dollars for the endowment. At 5% interest (remember, this was 1954) it would double in 20 years. The principle would never be used. Let me write a proposal and send it to you". That's the way it was left. I sent a

three page proposal within a few days. There were many contacts made with Mr. Christy, but the visit to the campus in August was special. Mrs. Beech loaned her Cadillac for the trip to Winfield from Wichita, and Emil Holgerson was the driver. There was the luncheon at the president's home, and a tour of the campus which ended at my office. I had a picture of the administration building and I said to Mr. Christy, "If you accept our proposal, we would name the building for you - Christy Administration Building. He thought for a moment or two and then said, "The only way for a bachelor to perpetuate his name is to put it on a building."

The committment didn't come until several months later. But, at last, he did sign the proposal in his bank office in Scott City and Allen Felt witnessed it. I want to insert here that we were vacationing with the family in Boulder, Colorado, and I had one of my hunches. I knew Mr. Felt was in Scott City; I had the feeling that we needed to see Mr. Christy together. I called Allen and told him I was taking the night train out of Denver and he said he would meet me. It was 3:00 a.m.! Allen and I worked out our strategy, called Mr. Christy the next morning, and met him at the bank.* Helen and the children drove from Boulder that day, and Monday morning we headed home. I learned that weekend that when I felt a strong urge to act, I'd better do it immediately! Riding on the train that Saturday night I wrote the inscription for the plaque that is at the entrance of Christy Administration Building today.

Sam Wallingford, graduate of Southwestern in 1908 and a loyal member of the board of trustees, had said to me, "If you get Ben to accept that half million dollar challenge, I'll give you $100,000".

* Mr. Christy signed the original proposal for $500,000 and Allen Felt and I witnessed it.

AN IMPORTANT TAX INCENTIVE DISCOVERED

Early in January of 1955, Emil Holgerson, Allen Felt and I pondered how Ben Christy could give storage wheat as a partial payment on his half-million dollar pledge to the college. Allen remembered a "Food Train" going through Kansas gathering up wheat for a Third World nation. Drew Pearson had written an article about the project. This sparked our thinking. Emil got in touch with the Treasury Department of Washington. They replied, "Yes, commodities could be given for charitable purposes." The advantage would be two-fold; tax wise the commodity would not be cash income, as long as it was not sold. The institution would sell the commodity and the credit for the gift would go to the donor. Thus it became a double tax break.

This tax ruling appeared in the Prentiss Hall Tax Guide and in the Internal Revenue Bulletin Number 11, issued March 14, 1955. It is stated in the accompanying letter which we sent to many friends of the college. People took advantage of this program, but none as much as Ben Christy.

Winfield, Kansas

TO FRIENDS OF SOUTHWESTERN COLLEGE,

GREETINGS:

A recent Internal Revenue regulation has provided a tax benefit of interest to you. Your tax attorney may refer to Internal Revenue Bulletin No. 11, issued under the date of March 14, 1955 for details.

Tax benefits as follows:

By donating a commodity from your farm, or place, its value is NOT considered income to you but it is allowable as a deduction for a contribution to the college up to the 30% limitation as provided in the code.

Commodity such as wheat, oats, (either in bushels or warehouse receipts), etc.; cattle, sheep, etc.; oil, hay, or any other commodity raised on your place, or within your share, may be given. Cost of producing the commodity item must be removed from deductible business expense or inventory costs.

DO NOT SELL the commodity and then give the money if you wish to take advantage of this tax benefit. Should you sell it then it becomes income to you and must be included and reported as such. However, by giving the college the commodity and letting the college sell it you have not realized income and therefore do not include it in your income items. This distinction is important.

The college will sell the commodity and issue a receipt for the value of the same. This gives you the amount to be listed among your donations.

As to Procedure:

Believing the above information and opportunity benefits you and the college we are happy to send it on to you for your consideration. Use the form suggested below (or simply write us a letter) and mail it to us. We shall inform you how we propose to handle the gift.

C. Orville Strohl, President   J. Lester Hankins, Vice President

- -

TO SOUTHWESTERN COLLEGE, Winfield, Kansas   Date_____ 19____

I/We hereby assign and set over to Southwestern College the following described commodity:

_____
(Bushels, or truck load, or number of stock, Warehouse Receipt No.(s)

We understand that you will acknowledge this gift by issuing an official receipt showing the value figure of the commodity hereby given to Southwestern College, Winfield, Kansas

Name_____   Address_____

Mail to the President or Vice President, Southwestern College, Winfield, Kansas

)Please send me ___ form(s) for future commodity gifts to Southwestern College)

62

Maybe he thought it couldn't be done, I'll never know. But I went to Wichita a few days after that proposal was signed, and received Sam's check for $100.000!!

A man in Detroit owned an apartment house in Arkansas City and wanted to dispose of it. He gave it to the college as a tax benefit. It was appraised at $30,000. So, on October 31, 1955, the Winfield Daily Courier announced that Southwestern College had received $630,000 in gift money from three donors. This amount, added to the Broadhurst gift of $300,000 totaled almost a million dollars! As a matter of fact, it reached over a million dollars because the alumni raised $50,000 at that time, and the president's home had cost $40,000.

By this time we had put together a huge 75th Anniversary program for the college.*   We had six years and our goal was $6,810,000.

Lester Hankins, pastor of the Methodist Church in Wellington, replaced Wendell Williams as Vice-President for Development.

Mr. and Mrs. J.M. Willson of Floydada, Texas, who were great admirers of Roy L. Smith, established the Smith-Willson lectureship in honor of Roy. (Roy graduated from Southwestern in 1908 along with Sam Wallingford) The first five lectures were given in 1955 by Roy, and the Willsons were present. This program is well endowed and will continue over the years. Its purpose is to enhance the life of the campus and pull together some facets of the liberal arts education that is often fragmented. The whole campus joined for these lectures, townspeople were invited and the auditorium was full. If a campus is to become a "Community", we all need to share some common experiences. These lectures often became the basis for class-room discussions.

* See brochure in file marked, "Printed Material".

A NEW IDEA FOR THE LIBRARY

In February of 1954 I attended an education meeting in Nashville, Tenn. While there we toured the Abingdon Cokesbury Press, which is the largest religious book publisher in the world. In March of that same year I received a request from our college librarian for additional funds for the purchase of books. We had no extra money.

Walking home that evening at about 6:00 p.m. I passed our library, silhouetted against the western sky. I thought about Methodism's great publishing house in Nashville, and our small library in need of books. An idea!! The next morning I wrote to our publishers and laid our need before them. Much to my surprise they replied immediately; they'd had such a plan, but the colleges had neglected to use it. They would provide books upon requisition, not including Bibles or Hymnals. We started the plan again and over 126 Methodist colleges profited from it. The publishing house notified the colleges and we received new books free for several years because of our connection with the Methodist church.

63

Student enrollment in 1954 was 330; it increased gradually and hit 745 in 1966-67.*

Arthur Covey was a student in the days of the Academy. He took art classes from Edith Dunlevy, the only boy in a class of girls. After class one day he walked across the campus with Mrs. Dunlevy and said, " I guess art is for girls and not for boys". She responded by saying, " If God wants you to be an artist and has given you the talents, you should never give up your dream". He stayed and eventually became one of America's first class artists, using watercolor, oil and lithograph. He did a number of murals, and one of his first pieces hangs in Southwest National Bank in Wichita. The mural was done for the old library and the bank bought it, placed it in the bank and had it re-touched to its original beauty.

I wrote to Mr. Covey and told him about the fire at the college in 1950. The campus was absolutely bare of art. I invited him to send a painting to his alma mater in honor of Edith Dunlevy, who was still living in Winfield at that time. He did just that. It is a beautiful work entitled, 'Autumn in New England'. The year was 1957. When it arrived, Mrs. Dunlevy was asked to help decide where it should hang, and she replied that it should hang in the presidents home. "It will be seen by more people there than anywhere else". And that is where it is still being enjoyed.

*   Enrollment from 1953 to 1970 was as follows:

1953 - 377	1964 - 663
1954 - 330	1965 - 716
1956 - 575	1966 - 748
1958 - 569	1967 - 672
1959 - 569	1968 - 701
1960 - 621	1969 - 665
1963 - 702	1970 - 705

64

In 1959 when we were building the Roy L. Smith College and Student Center, I again wrote to Mr. Covey. In addition to the Student Center there was Wallingford Hall and Shriwise Apartments, making three new buildings in all. Mr. Covey wrote, " I am getting ready to retire and would like to send the residue of my art works to Southwestern to be used in your new buildings". This was great news and we invited the Coveys to be present at Commencement in 1960 and present the art collection.

In April of 1960, Mr. Covey died in his sleep. So, Mrs. Covey, known professionally as Lois Lenski, was present at Commencement and made the presentation for her husband.* It was at the Baccalaureate service, and at that time our three Methodist churches cooperated in the 10:30 a.m. service. This service was held in Stewart Gymnasium.

Mrs. Covey was an author of note in her own right. Her field was children's books, which she illustrated with her own art. She also did lithographs. In 1968 Helen and I visited her in her home at Tarpon Springs, Florida. We presented to her an honorary Doctor of Literature degree, which had been authorized by the faculty and board of trustees.

THE TRIANGULAR CONCEPT

Early in my administration I decided that the greatest need facing Southwestern was not money, students, buildings or endowment. It was a psychological problem. There was money available if we could get it. There are young people wanting a college education - etc. If we could

* See catalogue of Covey Collection in notebook.

convince people - if they could be "sold" - develop strong convictions toward the college - make positive committments in behalf of our program. They needed to be able to visualize the campus - have concrete examples of what we were talking about.

Therefore, I published every year an illustrated report of our growth. These reports are on file in a folder marked as such. It was out of this struggle to create an image, that I developed the triangular concept of development. We used this in reports to Alumni, Foundations, townspeople and other publics. We had this triangle produced on large posters, slides and handouts. Finally, the idea began to soak through that there was a relationship between - Endowment - Buildings - Enrollment and Faculty. On the next page I have reproduced a page from my 1968 annual report.* Everyone could see the growth of the endowment as the base expanded (dark squares) and they could see how much was still needed (light squares). The rule of thumb was $10,000 for each student. Because of inflation, that goal would need to be doubled or even more today.

Below I have listed in sequence the buildings that resulted in a new campus:

1954 - Broadhurst Hall for men. (100 student capacity) $325,000 cost.

1954 - Kibbie Conference Room. This was done in recognition of Henry Kibbie's financial support through the years. He had given a fine new pipe organ for the auditorium in Richardson Hall. The organ was destroyed by the fire. The present organ was the gift of P.J. Sonner in 1953. The Executive Committee of the Board of Trustees uses this room every month and many policy decisions for the college are made in the Kibbie conference room.

* The idea was developed in 1960.

the triangular concept of development

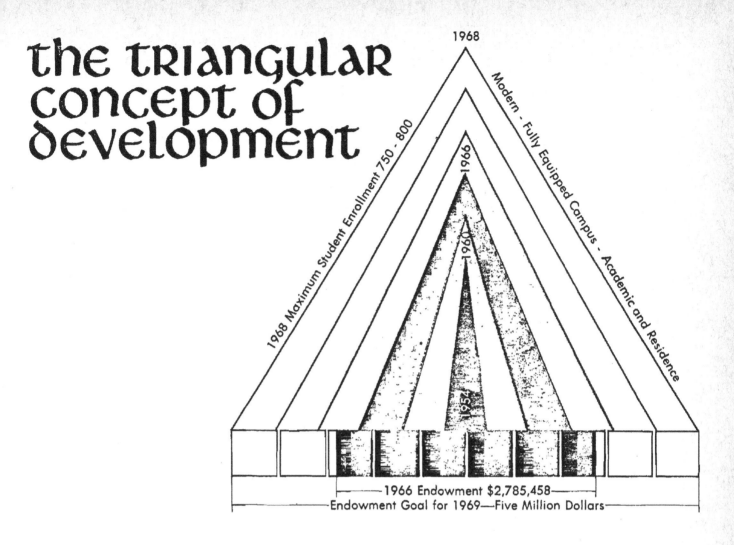

1968

1968 Maximum Student Enrollment 750 - 800

Modern - Fully Equipped Campus - Academic and Residence

1966

1960

1957

—1966 Endowment $2,785,458—
Endowment Goal for 1969—Five Million Dollars

The growth pattern of Southwestern College is best described by the triangle. The three sides represent:

- ALERT STUDENTS ON A RESIDENTIAL CAMPUS,
- A CAMPUS WELL EQUIPPED FOR LEARNING AND LIVING,
- ENDOWMENT TO SUPPORT A CAPABLE AND DEDICATED FACULTY.

In the past ten years over two million, two hundred thousand dollars has been added to the endowment. In the next three years we must raise $2,700,000. (Each square equals $500,000.)

Fifty-one carefully selected alumni are co-chairmen of estate planning. These persons are leaders in estate planning. Wise Christian stewardship comes alive in your *will* as you remember your alma mater. Estate planning has become a *must* factor in these days. *Remember Southwestern College in your will.*

For additional information regarding all phases of estate planning, write to Mr. J. W. Flaming, Director of Financial Development at Southwestern College, Winfield, Kansas.

65B

WE FOLLOWED these principles CAREFULLY

A QUARTERLY LETTER TO TRUSTEES OF CHURCH-RELATED INSTITUTIONS OF HIGHER LEARNING

August 1955   VOL. 11, No. 3

Ten Investment Principles

1.

Safety of the principal should be the primary factor in the choice of investments for an endowment fund; maximum income over long periods is important but should be secondary to the preservation of the principal.

2.

Diversification of investments is important. They should be distributed so as not to have a disproportionate amount in any one class of investment, type of industry or business, geographical location—or too many maturing in a single period. Ordinarily the fund should have a balanced distribution between fixed income securities (bonds, mortgages, preferred stocks, and similar items) and those (common stocks) having variable returns and with a reasonable possibility of appreciation in value. Where several different funds are held by an institution, the investments should be merged, whenever possible, to facilitate management and provide broader diversification.

3.

Securities, generally speaking, should be selected from lists of marketable securities published by exchanges such as the New York Exchange and subject to ready sale if and when sales are necessary. Caution is urged in the investing of endowment funds in the securities of local corporations whose securities have limited marketability.

4.

Endowment funds of a church-related educational institution should never knowingly be invested in enterprises out of accord with the general social aims of the church.

5.

Investments should not be bought by or sold to a member of the institution's board of trustees or of its investment committee, or by or to an employee of the institution itself. The institution or its authorized representative should buy and sell securities only through qualified brokers.

6.

Profits on the sale of investment assets should be treated as capital gains and become a part of the corpus of the fund. Such profits should never be used for current expenses. No endowment funds should be expended, nor pledged as collateral for loans, to pay the institution's current expenses.

7.

Endowment funds should never be invested in the nonincome-producing plant facilities of the college; nor in income-producing plant units of the college unless "yes" is the unqualified answer to the question, "Would this investment be approved if our institution were not involved?" Neither should the investment of permanent funds be made in the form of a loan or mortgage to any institution or individual where necessary action in enforcing collection would prove embarrassing.

8.

Assets received as gifts should be evaluated promptly, and those that do not meet the committee's standards for purchase or are undesirable for other reasons should either be sold immediately or earmarked for sale at acceptable prices. Proper recognition should be taken of the interests of the donor, as well as the interests of the college, in the sale of such assets.

9.

Investment responsibilities, including an established measure of authority, should rest with an investment committee comprised of members appointed by and responsible to the board of trustees who, because of ability and experience, are qualified to handle the institution's trust funds. The investment committee with the approval of the board of trustees should obtain the services of competent and disinterested investment counsel not engaged in the buying or selling of securities.

10.

A custodian agreement providing for the deposit of all securities should be made with a bank or trust company having adequate safety deposit facilities.

COMMISSION ON HIGHER EDUCATION—NATIONAL COUNCIL—CHURCHES OF CHRIST—U.S.A.
257 FOURTH AVENUE, NEW YORK 10, N. Y.

TRUSTEE

66

1955 - <u>Kirk Circle Drive</u>, paved and curbed with an attractive silver-
dale stone sign at the entrance of the campus in recognition
of the ten years Dr. Kirk served as president.

1955 - <u>Presidents Residence</u>. The building and grounds committee
surveyed the campus carefully to decide where the new home was
to be built. Some suggested that it should be off campus. I
insisted that it should be on the campus and become a part of
the <u>residential campus</u>. This location has been used to great
advantage through the years. Student receptions, faculty
group dinners, open houses, off campus events, Christmas events,
etc. have proven that the choice was right. Cost $40,000.+

1956 - <u>Lois Hill Memorial Chapel</u>. This chapel was made possible by
Dr. and Mrs. Ward Cole in memory of Mrs. Cole's sister, who had
been employed by the college for a number of years before her
death.

1956 - <u>Christy Administration Building</u> completed and dedicated. The
original building was made possible by a banker in McPherson.
The new building was named for a banker in Scott City, 50 years
later. Present for the dedication of the new building were Sam
Wallingford, Olive Ann Beech, Bill Broadhurst, the board of
trustees and many, many others. The auditorium was full.

1958 - <u>Sutton Hall</u> located on the corner of Warren and McCabe streets.
Warren and McCabe were both Bishops of the Methodist church. The
building was constructed when government loans were 3%. Later,
Mrs. Sutton gave us funds to pay off the loan and a Section of
land in Wichita county, which was placed in the endowment. Mrs.
Sutton lived in St. John, Kansas (Capacity of 70 men, cost of $285,000).

1960* - <u>Wallingford</u> <u>Hall</u> for women. Lounges, apartments, laundry, etc. (Capacity of 147 women)

1960* - <u>Roy</u> <u>L.</u> <u>Smith</u> <u>College</u> <u>and</u> <u>Student</u> <u>Center</u>. The building is not a student union. It was designed to be a gathering place for campus friends and students and off-campus people, including parents, townspeople, alumni, etc. That was the basis of its name.

1960* - <u>Shriwise</u> <u>Student</u> <u>Apartments</u>, named for Christina Shriwise, benefactor of the college in money and farm land.

1960* - <u>Honor</u> <u>Dormitory</u> ..... on the North side of the campus (two sections).

1961 - <u>John</u> <u>and</u> <u>Sherlah</u> <u>King</u> provided the funds for the new driveway strectching from Warren Street to Fowler Street. Both Warren and Fowler were bishops of the Methodist church.

1962 - <u>Monypeny</u> <u>Cinder</u> <u>Track</u> with a 220 yard runway, named for Mr. W.W. Monypeny, longtime track coach at the college. Cost $12,000.

1964 - <u>Helen</u> <u>Graham</u> <u>Theater</u>, named for the distinguished teacher and drama coach ..... founder of <u>Campus</u> <u>Players</u>. Cost $8,000.

1965 - <u>Darbeth</u> <u>Fine</u> <u>Arts</u> <u>Center</u> ..... including <u>Messenger</u> <u>Recital</u> <u>Hall</u>, named for Elizabeth Thompson Wells and Darwin Wells, both of whom are graduates, benefactors and trustees. Messenger was Mrs. Gertrude Wallingford's maiden name. This hall was made possible by an estate gift. Cost was $785,000.00 (Including parking lots)

---

* These four buildings cost over $1,492,000, with a furnishing cost of $95,000. Great care was spent in deciding on their location. Great 'cats' tore out the South side of the hill where the student center is located. The drive to the hill used to go in front of the administration building. It was closed and a new drive developed. The entire campus was turned around.

I flew in a private plane (Perry Bemis' father being the pilot) to Hobbs, New Mexico to visit with Roy L. Smith about naming the center for him. The conference put $200,000 into this project. The tri-dining area is named for Roy's father and mother. I asked him what I should say about his mother ....and he said, "She prayed her dreams into reality". His father.... he said ..... "He was a friend of the young". The plaque carries these words.

Mr. & Mrs. Byron Waite named the Home Economics dept. on

Founder's Day, 1963. A list of all endowments, including the above,

was published each year with family names and the project,

such as scholarships or unrestricted endowments.

OTHER ADVANCES MADE IN ACADEMICS

1954-72 - Library acquistions increased from 28,600 volumns to 80,000.

1967-72 - Seniors graduaded number 2,193.

1967 -   Graduate program established with Oklahoma City University.

1972 -   Government grant establishing the Winfield Cooperating Colleges,

which has continued for ten years.

1960-72 - Four endowded faculty Chairs established:
One is chemistry honoring Professor Oncley.
One in Mathematics honoring Professor John Phillips.
One in Physics honoring Dr. Penrose Albright.
One in Business Administration honoring Olive Ann Beech,
   long time Trustee and benefactor.

These endowments are still open to receive contributions

from donors who have a special interest in these programs.

1972 -   The Orville and Helen Strohl scholarship endowment in recog-

nition of the 18½ years that the Strohls spent on the campus

as President and first lady. This endowment has reached

$30,000 plus and is being added to each year.

1972 -   The total endowment has reached 4,500,000. The Reid estate

amounting to 2 million dollars was added later plus other

estates that had been developed between 1954-1972. The endow-

ment now stands in excess of 11,000,000 dollars.

Much of the Reid estate had been given to us as a life estate during

my administration, especially the land in Edwards, Pratt and Stafford

Counties. The College still owns this land and now it is producing

oil - 80% going into reserves and 20% being used for budgets.

* This summary was published in The Southwesterner of May, 1972.

70

PURPOSE RESTATED WITH CONVICTIONS

The decade of the 60's have already gone down in history as being ten years of revolution & upheaval. So many influences converged upon those years- the war - the divisions of attitude in America because there was never a declaration of war - student riots - unrest on campuses and then the Kent State students confronting the law which resulted in several students being killed. Presidents were driven from office, buildings were taken over, sit-ins, and in some cases, bombing of campus buildings. None of us knew who might be next or what might happen. Every once-in-awhile we got word of planned raids on our campus but they never took place.

I kept the door of my office open all the time. The psychology was positive. The President's Advisory Committee, consisting of a cross section of people, including students, kept in touch with the situation. There were several times when I met with large groups of students in the Student Center. I visited the dormitories for informal chats. Smaller groups would come to the President's home in the evenings. Beneath it all there was a serious effort to think through the place of a church related (Methodist) college. Students read the social creed of Methodism & wondered why their college wasn't crusading for social justice. These were the years when Martin Luther King was in the headlines almost every other day. We did have small groups, accompanied by the Chaplain, go to Selma and elsewhere to help in voter registration.

So it became evident that we had to produce a careful statement of Convictions upon which Southwestern was developed.

71

CONVICTIONS UPON WHICH
SOUTHWESTERN COLLEGE IS DEVELOPED

I.

Historically, the academic community has been unique among all other institutions. It has been a place for learning organized by an association of persons having certain powers, rights, duties, and purposes concerning higher education which usually results in the awarding of degrees.

Likewise, historically, such an academic community has been allowed to go about its business of teaching and learning, setting standards, awards, and punishments free from outside interference. In such a community greater freedom and/or greater restrictions may prevail than in society at large; and of course, these have been fixed by the educational community itself.

A college or university is not an agency of action to transform society in behalf of a cause no matter how exalted that cause may be.

A college is not a political party, nor an experiment in sociology, nor an attack on poverty nor on civil rights.

The moment it becomes such it loses its independence and objectivity and subjects itself to curbs and controls on the part of society.

This is not to say that the academic community is not to concern itself with social quality, social criticism, and social reform, and to pursue the truth wherever it may lead.

This is where academic freedom is needed -- and such freedom cannot survive if the university becomes an instrument of revolution.

The academic community must be free to argue, to debate, to dissent, and to express unorthodox views. The right of private judgment is a basic right for all Americans, and especially for the campus. It must have the right to make qualitative, intellectual judgment without fear of civil interference. The search for truth -- free and unfettered -- must be protected with all our might.

II.

Southwestern College is committed, from stem to stern, to be an Olympic winner in the field of higher education that excels in the liberal arts.

Such an aspiration has demanded and shall continue to demand -- Vision! Energy! Money! All of these are hard to come by.

72

III. <u>VISION</u>!

Strong colleges grow quietly and solidly over many years, gathering unto theirselves <u>institutional strength</u>. Strength that comes from many factors that are interwoven in the fabric of our lives.

Integrity, honesty, and respect lie in the core of such campuses in great abundance.

The great areas of thought in the exciting pattern of the liveral arts include the place of religion in the development of man and civilization. It includes the social and natural sciences, communications, languages, and the fine arts.

It has <u>historical roots</u> that recognize the yesterdays.
It has <u>experimental programs</u> that penetrate the tomorrows,
It has <u>self-criticism</u> that saves us from repeating mistakes.

It practices the <u>art of democracy</u> which encourages responsible behavior, the freedom of thought, the right of private judgment, and respect for individuals.

It <u>recognizes</u> that every human being is a miracle of creation -- who possesses unlimited potential.

If there is a <u>future for man</u> and his creative role in the affairs of an ever-expanding universe, <u>then there is a future for colleges like South-western.</u>

IV.

Most colleges <u>let things happen</u> instead of <u>making things happen</u>. Southwestern College need not become the victim of the present -- neither do we need to become locked into contemporary crises. We have the nerve, courage, and faith. <u>Our motivations are based upon the quality of our mission.</u>

<u>All of us within the academic community establish our goals, develop our plans, and reach solutions to our most pressing needs. This develops muscle and toughness of mind, spirit, and willpower</u> among us. This justifies our continued existence as a college.

V.

<u>Southwestern College</u> -- is not a custodian of the old order, a perpetuator of the proven, or a curator of the present. This College is an open-ended venture -- <u>selective of the past</u> -- <u>a creative critic of the present oriented toward the tomorrows.</u>

73

THE KENT STATE KILLINGS

The Kent State College turmoil and killing of several students was a shock to every campus and all students in the late 1960's. Our students were saddened, angry and upset. The killings took place on Friday.

Saturday night a group of men students from Broadhurst Hall came to the Presidents home to see me. They said, "We must do something to show that we are concerned". "That's good," I said. "What do you have in mind?" "We plan to make three large black floats on wheels to head a parade of students and faculty and go down 9th Street to Main and hold a meeting at 9th and Main." "We want your permission."

"If that is the best that you can come up with, it will be approved." "But let me point out that your parade will go right by the high school and the students will be there watching." "Three large black floats, what will they think?" I asked if this was the best that college students could come up with. It was negative and made me think of a funeral. I suggested that they be more creative and positive. "Why don't you consider doing something that would interpret the basic cause of such a tragedy?" "Why is this happening, what can we do to correct it?" "Think it over and let me know."

Sunday afternoon they came back with a totally different attitude. They wanted to get the larger churches involved. They did at the Methodist, Baptist and Presbyterian churches as well as some smaller ones. They met with the youth groups, pastors and some laymen.

74

Then on Monday morning at 10:00 a.m., with the cooperation of the whole campus, an assembly was held. Students spoke, the Chaplain, a faculty member, as well as several others. The tone of the whole affair was changed. The bottom line was something like this. "Three Students at Kent State have been denied their education because of their assassination in this unfortunate riot. Let us help make it possible for 3 young people who want a college education, to attend Southwestern. Let us establish a scholarship program to be entitled: "The Kent State Living Scholarships".

Offering plates were at the doors to receive funds. The Winfield Courier carried the announcement. Students called on many people in town in behalf of the program. Trustees and parents contributed and the fund grew to a very respectable size. The story of this program was written up and distributed widely.

Students will respond in a positive way if challenged. Three black floats-- No! Living Scholarships-- Yes!

Four Development Programs 1954-74

There are several ways of measuring a college. I always said we had three years in one. There was the academic year (Sept.-May); the financial year (July-June) and the calendar year.

The thrust that gives a college a sense of direction and movement is usually related to the kind of Development Program to which the college was commited. In these 18½ years these were 4 and I list them with some detail below:

1. The 75th Anniversary Program   1955-1960
2. The Great Issues   1960-1963

75

3. The Master Plan   1963-1968

4. Commitment to Achievement   1969-1974

(1) The Goals of the 75th Anniversary program encompassed a total of $6,810,000. It included debt retirement, faculty salaries, small chapel and organ in the administration building, endowment, buildings, (Presidents home, girls dormitory and student center, described on page 66) and budget requirements.

It called upon Alumni, faculty, Trustees, churches, corporations and business, foundations and the local community to help lift the load. Each group was given a specific goal.

The brochure spelled out the purpose of the college (described on page 54) and the program was endorsed by such persons as Olive Ann Beech, Bishop Dana Dawson, Sam P. Wallingford, William Broadhurst, Ronald Meredith, Adel Throckmorton, Dale Dunlap and Myrne Richards, a student.

UNIVERSITY SENATE SURVEY

The University Senate of the Methodist Church is the oldest accrediting agency in America. We invited the Senate to make this study and inventory of Southwestern. A doctor (M.D.) gives a person a physical to be sure they are in good health, and, if not, to correct what they are doing so that good health is assured. So, on this special anniversary, we wanted such an analysis made. Seven men, strong educators from several universities, spent three days on campus in November, 1959. The written report was presented to the Trustees

and faculty in March of 1960. Their recommendations became the basis of our second development program.

THE CELEBRATION OF 75 YEARS

FOUNDERS DAY, MARCH 7-8.

Theme: "Old Enough To Be Proven"

Speaker (Convocation) - Dr. Lewis M. Simes '09, Michigan School Of Law

Noon Luncheon - Bishop F. Gerald Ensley, Iowa

Birthday Cake - 2:30 - "Education is Everybody's Business"

Campus Tours - Reception for all by faculty at 4:30; Campus Players production by Helen Graham depicting Southwestern's 75 years, 1885-1960.

SPECIAL CONVOCATION, CONCERT AND WORKSHOP, APRIL 19-20.

Speaker (Convocation) - Dr. Emory Lindquist

Organ Concert - Dr. Arthur Poister, Syracuse University

Following Day - Master Class, conducted by Dr. Poister, followed by a reception.

COMMENCEMENT, May 28-29.

Featuring Dr. Elton Trueblood, Earlham College. Special alumni features.

SMITH-WILLSON LECTURESHIP, NOVEMBER 9-11.

Special Lecturer - Dean Howard Thurman, Boston University.

Theme - "Disciplines Of The Spirit" (These lectures were later published in a book under that title.)

HOMECOMING, NOVEMBER 12.

Re-enacting the "Building Of The Mound," at the evening dinner.

IN 1885

76A

Old North Hall—1885

Christy Hall—1960

Southwestern was started on her way. Through the years she has kept her vision, and with pride and integrity she has now fulfilled 75 years of her responsibilities.

Thus 75 years of heroic struggle, hardships of pioneer days, and remarkable achievement become a matter of record in the annals of Kansas history. Today Southwestern stands on the threshold of a great new opportunity—She is

Old enough to be proven!
Young enough to be contemporary!
Strong enough to challenge!

Southwestern's progress is reported in the following pages.

75th Anniversary Report

Southwestern College

| ... Templar, ... nt | Joe R. Everly, Executive Committee Chairman | R. Byron Waite, Finance Committee Chairman | Olive Ann Beech, Endowment Committee Chairman | Cautious A. Choate, Personnel Committee Chairman | Lyman S. Johnson, Degrees Committee Chairman | W. W. Keith, Property and Insurance Committee Chairman | Clarence H. Hamm, Residence Committee Chairman |

—1960—

Dr. Paul H. Davis, Educational Consultant, says:

"After visiting forty colleges and universities I found two items which appeared to me to be paramount in all the exceptional institutions. Succinctly they were: (1) clearly defined objectives and (2) missionary zeal.

"A year later, after visiting an additional forty colleges and universities, I found another factor which is common to exceptional colleges, and it may be a factor which ranks above all others. It is this: EXCEPTIONAL COLLEGES EITHER HAVE OR HAVE HAD EXCEPTIONAL TRUSTEES.

"That was found to be true in each of the exceptional colleges and universities of the eighty which I have visited—every one. By the adjective 'exceptional' I mean to designate those institutions which are outstanding in their rate of progress toward THEIR objectives."

SOUTHWESTERN COLLEGE PROUDLY PRESENTS HER DISTINGUISHED TRUSTEES!

77

(2) THE GREAT ISSUES (2nd DEVELOPMENT PROGRAM)

The Ten Great Issues for 1960-65 were as follows:

A. Endowment (Triangular Concept)

B. Faculty Salary Goals

C. Academic Blueprint - establishing programs for Sabbatical Leave and Doctoral Completion.

D. Kresge Foundation Challenge of $20,000.00

E. Southwestern and World Affairs.

F. Campus expansion by 30 acres to the East.

G. New Fine Arts Center.

H. New Women's Residence Hall.

I. New Men's Residence Hall.

J. Naming gifts for major projects.

Total goal for the above projects was $4,210,400.

(3) THE MASTER PLAN, 1963-68
("The Great Issues" were merged into a "Master Plan" and extended to 1968)

Purpose: To strengthen Southwestern's total achievement by raising educational and financial objectives to keep pace with the times. Total of $5,250,000.

This total was broken down into thirteen projects, which are spelled out in brochures. Several days were spent with alumni, students, trustees, faculty and administration as we took the recommendations of the University Senate Survey to develop this program.

NEXT FLIGHT UP

Annual Report

The "President" is the symbol of the institution that he serves. Southwestern College has climbed the *first half* of the five-year program laid out in 1963, known as THE MASTER PLAN. We are now on the *second flight up*.

C. Orville Strohl

PURPOSE

of

STERN COLLEGE

is

BECOME

NTIAL COLLEGE

T OF BEAUTY

E OF CULTURE

WHERE

Y EDUCATION

RTED FROM THE

POINT OF VIEW

•

that flourish best are
vigorously declare their
d live by them."

—Arnold W. Stoke
arican College President"

What We Believe

In fulfilling its role as a church-related, liberal arts college, Southwestern seeks to provide an atmosphere of Christian inspiration and intellectual stimulation with a professionally trained and dedicated faculty and adequate physical facilities.

Southwestern is an independent college (non-tax supported) and as such is in line with a historic trend stemming from the Middle Ages, the Renaissance, and the Reformation.

Christian higher education, free from the domination of government, is essential to human freedom and democracy. The Christian college gives rise to Christian culture and preserves its dynamic character.

When the highest quality of the liberal arts is given purpose and illumination by Christianity at its best, and when a campus is MOVED and MOTIVATED and inspired by a faith in the Christian theme of things, and when a commitment to God is the source of all truth—there you have CHRISTIAN HIGHER EDUCATION in action.

A great college is a spirit—a mood—an atmosphere that transcends men and money and materials. Dignity, freedom, and reponsibilities characterize its campus. It is a living, human, and growing thing. It is a web of personal relationships permeated by a sense of dedication and loyalty to the best in life.

The destiny of our world depends upon a universal commitment to education —not merely to solve our immediate problems like bulging enrollments, inadequate teacher salaries, curriculum upheavals, etc.—but to endow our people with knowledge, imagination, flexibility, and dedication to the moral and philosophical foundations of democracy and to Christian values. Education is no longer an adjunct to civilization. It is rather, the base from which all important problems are to be attacked. Its role is as vital in this great expanding century as it was when Kansas was a territory, and our country was a struggling emergent nation.

Therefore this is not only a time for education, but for GREATNESS in education. Greatness lies in a people who are intellectually masterful, spiritually sound, as well as technically trained and skilled.

We believe that in the providence of Almighty God Southwestern College is destined to face, with humility, but with courage, the unheralded future as a great Christian liberal arts college.

C. Orville Strohl
President

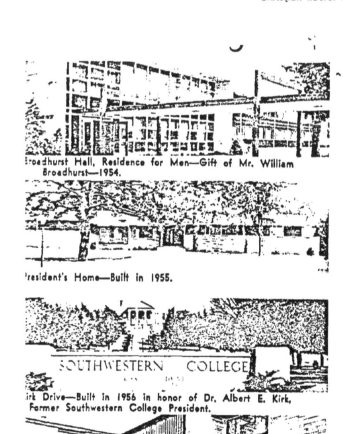

Broadhurst Hall, Residence for Men—Gift of Mr. William Broadhurst—1954.

President's Home—Built in 1955.

SOUTHWESTERN COLLEGE

irk Drive—Built in 1956 in honor of Dr. Albert E. Kirk, Former Southwestern College President.

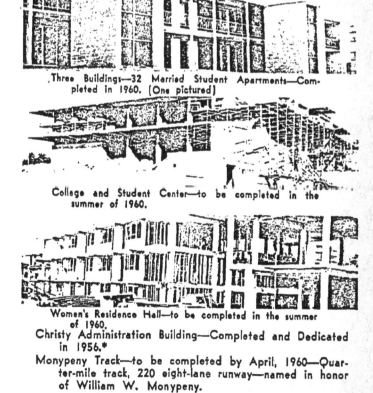

Three Buildings—32 Married Student Apartments—Completed in 1960. (One pictured)

College and Student Center—to be completed in the summer of 1960.

Women's Residence Hall—to be completed in the summer of 1960.

Christy Administration Building—Completed and Dedicated in 1956.*

Monypeny Track—to be completed by April, 1960—Quarter-mile track, 220 eight-lane runway—named in honor of William W. Monypeny.

*Completion included the Lois Hall Memorial Chapel, classrooms, and administrative offices.

78

(4) COMMITMENT TO ACHIEVEMENT, 1969-1974

By this time, the balance of the above programs, which was
basically endowment, was gathered up with this last Advance. This
program was to reach through to 1974 but Sam Wallingford died very
suddenly in New York City in November of 1968 at age 84. Soon we
learned of a codicil that he had written on October 15, 1968, which
said, "I give and bequeath to Southwestern College, Winfield, Kansas,
the sum of One Hundred and Fifty Thousand Dollars ($150,000),
provided that within three years from the date of my death, the college
shall raise One Million Five Hundred Thousand Dollars ($1,500,000) in
cash, bona fide pledges, and irrevocable bequests."
(Note: The codicil was written only one month before Sam's death.)

In reality, the development program now was limited to only
three years, 1969-1972, to fit Mr. Wallingford's challenge. Into
this "slot of time" the college was to have regular ten year surveys
by the North Central Association of Colleges And Universities.

There remained two major building projects, the library expansion
and a physical education building for women, including a co-educational
swimming pool. Cora White Stone of Wellington died, leaving a bequest
to the college of $500,000. (The announcement was made stating the
figure to be $400,000, but when the securities were liquidated, they
amounted to the larger figure.) So, a government loan of 3% plus
$200,000 from her estate made possible these two projects. Two Hundred
Thousand Dollars was placed in the endowment, invested in Wisconsin
Electric Bonds (maturity in 30 years). The 7 7/8 % income took care

...to the trustees and the Probate Court of Sedgwick County, Kansas.

Section I
Cash for all purposes $1,091,946.62
Pledges   578,088.09
Property   11,427.71

Sub Total $1,681,462.42

Section II
Irrevocable bequests and other deferred giving $467,781.13

Grand Total $2,149,243.55

In addition to the irrevocable bequests shown above, there was a total of $1,067,900 in general wills written and reported to the college during these three years. Many deferred gifts will be coming to the college during the next 15 or 20 years.

This is a real success story for Southwestern College. We are deeply grateful to all of you who had a vital part in it:

Alumni, Faculty, Students, Friends, and Trustees
Foundations, Corporations, Business, and Industry
The Kansas West Conference of the United Methodist Church

Meanwhile, let us push on relentlessly to complete the "Commitment To Achievement" program which ends in June, 1974.

C. Orville Strohl
President of the College

THE WALLINGFORD

CHALLENGE

— $150,000

Southwestern College proudly announces it has met the requirements of the Wallingford Challenge and will receive the $150,000 which was a conditional bequest made by the late Sam P. Wallingford.

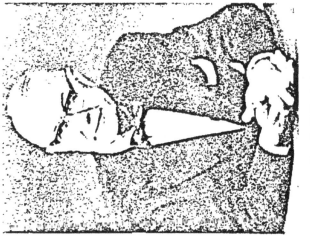

Sam P. Wallingford

Southwestern was challenged to secure $1,500,000 in cash, bona fide pledges, trusts, and irrevocable wills during three years from the time of Mr. Wallingford's death on November 18, 1968.

This was a tremendous challenge. It meant raising $100 for every $10—$1,000 for every $100. The college could not neglect other aspects of her long-range development program, "Commitment to Achievement".

In December of 1968, the trustees and I wrestled with the question concerning professional help. The decision was made that we should "do our own thing". A few of my responsibilities were shifted to the Dean of the College so that I could give as much time as possible to this herculean task. Alumni, trustees, faculty, students and friends of the college were notified of the job to be done and were asked to respond. Legal counsel was sought concerning irrevocable bequests and other matters pertaining to deferred gifts.

Mr. G. D. McSpadden, attorney, President Strohl, and Mr. J. W. Flaming, Director of Development, read the document which verifies the completion of the Wallingford Challenge.

of the government loan principle and interest, and in the end the
$200,000 would still be in endowment. This skillful handling of
these funds was worked out by Arthur Smith, George Templar working
with me, and was approved by the Executive Committee.

So, on June 30, 1972, we had buttoned up the program known as
Commitment To Achievement. The Wallingford challenge had been met.
It was the largest and hardest challenge that we had ever faced,
a total of $1,650,000 in three years. Helen and I could not think
of forging a new program. North Central had accredited Southwestern
for another ten years.

In September we had our usual freshman reception in the President's
home. We will always remember a young, aggressive freshman from Ohio
who came through the line. He said to me, "How long have you been
President of Southwestern?" I told him eighteen years. He stopped
short and replied in an astonished voice, "Why, that was before I
was born!" "Sure," I said, "we've been getting ready for you all
through these years, and I'm glad you have come." Later I said to
Helen, "This freshman startled me into realizing how long we have been
here. This is the time to terminate our work." And we did on June 30,
the end of our financial year. I announced our decision at the
November Executive Board Meeting. This gave the Trustees time to
search for a new president to take office on July 1, 1972. And they
did.

Attached is a resolution adopted by the Trustees at their March
meeting. I also insert an editorial that Mr. W. W. Keith, Publisher
of the Winfield Daily Courier, published on November 21, 1971.

80

RESOLUTION PRESENTED
BY
JUDGE GEORGE TEMPLAR

"Whereas, for a good many years, Southwestern College has had the good fortune to be blessed with leadership afforded it by Dr. C. Orville Strohl, one of its own graduates; his great faith, his infectious enthusiasm, his undaunted persistence, his vision of possibilities, which he brought into reality through untiring perseverance, has inspired all those with whom he worked to accomplish so much that is visible and apparent on this beautiful and attractive campus, we, as his friends and members of the Board of Trustees, are exceedingly proud of his achievements.

"Whereas, with great reluctance, we have, at his insistence, accepted his retirement from the executive leadership of this school, we take this opportunity to acknowledge the outstanding service he has provided in greatly increasing the endowments, the improvements of the scholastic standards, the vast improvement of the physical plant and the campus, and a wide variety of other accomplishments for which he is entitled to great commendation.

"Now, therefore, be it resolved, at our annual meeting assembled on the campus at Winfield, Kansas, that we, members of the Board of Trustees, on behalf of ourselves, the faculty, the students, the friends, and supporters of Southwestern College, note and express our deep appreciation for the long, dedicated, and effective service that he, together with his lovely wife, Helen, have given this college, and on this occasion, we express to them our wish that they will have and enjoy many years of good health and happiness and that they will seek and find an opportunity of lending their continued support to our causes.

"To these ends, we wish them both all the blessings and rewards to which they are so richly entitled. Our prayers and best wishes go with them." (Standing ovation)

> --- Motion made by Judge Templar, seconded by Dr. Borger, and carried, that the resolution be adopted and made a part of the minutes.

81

Winfield (Kan.) Daily Courier, Mon., Nov. 22, 1971

Courier Comment

Community Will Miss Strohl As College Leader

When Dr. C. Orville Strohl resigned as president of Southwestern College, he said, among other things, "A new, vigorous and dynamic leader, well qualified, can lead this college into areas of undreamed of excellence."

We are sure that Dr. Strohl believes this to be true and it is possible that this could happen, but if such a man is found, and Southwestern continues to progress, it can only be because of the foundation laid during Dr. Strohl's administration. When Orville Strohl came to Southwestern the college had an enrollment of a little more than 300 students. Its endowment was a meager $580,761.00; it had a campus valued at $1,961,947.00 that was woefully short of facilities to handle even its small student body.

Only a man with Dr. Strohl's vision, courage, confidence and faith in the future would have accepted the presidency. Today Southwestern has an endowment of $4,254,535.00. This is the largest of any church related school in Kansas and could be the largest factor in Southwestern's future. It is a fact of life that colleges without adequate endowment will probably not survive.

The campus now has ample facilities to provide for the students and allow for increased enrollment in the future. It is presently valued at $8,669,753.00.

These are all major accomplishments, but another area where Dr. Strohl has exerted great influence should be mentioned. This has been in the matter of faculty salaries and benefits. Dr. Strohl has worked tirelessly to maintain a superior faculty in the belief that academic excellence is the measure of a school. Under his regime faculty salaries and benefits have increased from $131,086.00 in 1954 to $676,014.00 at the present time. This is in contrast to some other schools who have hired faculty at whatever the going rate happened to be without regard for the future.

Southwestern has indeed been fortunate to have Orville Strohl as its president during these critical years. We hope that further progress will be recorded in the future.

In addition to his work at the college, Dr. Strohl has been an important asset to the community, serving on many civic boards and committees. We hope that whatever his plans for the future may be, he will consider remaining in Winfield in some capacity.

82

SOUTHWESTERN AND THE KANSAS WEST ANNUAL CONFERENCE

There have always been fine working relationships between the college and the conference. Each year the churches of the conference financially support their college. Many pastors take a positive attitude toward directing students to the campus. But, there are two major events that are worthy of remembering. The first one is referred to as the "CHECK" campaign, which meant --

CHRISTIAN HIGHER EDUCATION in CENTRAL KANSAS

This was an effort to raise 4½ million dollars within our conference, over a period of several years, for Kansas Wesleyan and Southwestern. These funds were to be used for endowment, as far as each college could manage. The final figures reached $2,100,000 for each college. Only $200,000 of our share went into the Roy L. Smith College and Student Center. Over $800,000 went into endowment. This "CHECK" program was a giant step for the churches of the conference. Raymond Dewey was General Chairman. We had a professional fund raiser and each college president assisted.

The second major event took place in October of 1965, the tenth anniversary of the Smith-Willson Lectureship. I recommended that we use these funds in an effort to search deeply for a Sense of Direction in Christian Higher Education. I have reproduced statements of my basic purpose, plus the names of the national leaders who were participants. It was a very successful and helpful program, as is stated by Dr. Joe Riley Burns and Professor Dennis Akin on the second page.

83

A Sense of Direction

How does a church-related college, composed of a strong faculty, alert and capable students, trustees who are men and women of affairs in today's business world, and ministers who are asked to support higher education, ever come to a common understanding regarding the purpose of their college?

This has been the basic question that has confronted me for the past decade. Each of these groups are deeply concerned. Yet seldom do they have the opportunity to even be together—let alone work together—digging deeply into the philosophical purposes that make our united efforts worthwhile.

Students want to know the purpose of their Alma Mater. The labors of the faculty are much more fruitful if they know the goals of their college. The dedication of the trustees will increase when they become convinced that the students and faculty are united in making their educational experiences meaningful and purposeful. Ministers of the protestant church rejoice in knowing that the church-related college is interested in remaining a strong arm of the church and that its objectives include the Christian liberal arts.

None of these groups can "tell" the others what must be done. There must be a climate of conversation among them.—directed especially at the purpose for our existence.

The ancient Greeks understood the art and courage of communication. They knew that the opposite point of view was important. Out of this climate came freedom of the mind and the process of communication that must be kept alive in every generation and especially ours.

They believed that the complex social problems are solved after careful examination and reasoning by thoughtful people. Greek civilization flourished as long as this climate lasted.

The dark ages are characterized chiefly by a breakdown of communication among the intelligentsia. Intellectual isolation is worse than physical separation.

The Renaissance saw the rebirth of communication in many forms—art, literature, music and conversation. Learning was advanced.

The mutual exchange of sound ideas is to the glory of mankind. The concepts of progress and the development of human dignity have meaning only insofar as we can talk about them—reach thoughtful conclusions regarding them, and determine patterns of actions and behavior to make them a reality.

And so in 1964 a committee of 18 was appointed by the Board of Trustees.

They were to find ways and means of bringing these several groups together so that we could take a real hard look at ourselves. Its membership was composed of students, faculty, trustees, ministers and laymen. They have had a number of meetings

In addition two faculty workshops explored ways and means to explore more deeply the philosophy underlying Christian Higher Education.

In October of 1965 the whole campus came alive as students, faculty, trustees, ministers, and laymen spent three days in a search for the basic concepts of the church-related college. Thus the Smith-Willson Lectures became a vital part of our study. Our quest was given direction by three major addresses by Dr. Ernest Colwell, President, School of Theology, Claremont, California; Dr. Myron F. Wicke, General Secretary, Division of Higher Education, Board of Education of the Methodist Church; Dr. Manning M. Pattillo, Director, Danforth Commission on Church Colleges and Universities of the Danforth Foundation; and Bishop W. McFerrin Stowe presented papers, led seminars and discussions.

The contents of this manual will set forth some of the highlights of our experience. We publish it in the hope that it will give to each of you a *"sense of direction"* in which Southwestern College is moving.

If you. . .

. . . are students now you have great interest in its contents.

. . . are a prospective student you will want to read this statement as well as other material regarding Southwestern College.

. . . are a parent this will give you better insight into what we believe is important.

. . . are a prospective donor you will be interested in this material because it tries to put into focus our major concerns.

are a faculty member at Southwestern or elsewhere you will have keen interest because this is the product of an academic community.

No statement arrived at by many groups remains in focus for long. A college that is alive is not static. . . . but keeps growing and changing. Therefore the Boards of Trustees have appointed a steering committee composed of these same four or five groups whose responsibilities are to develop a five year program based upon the findings and summaries of these studies.

C. O. Strohl

84

What Has This Week Meant?

Dr. Joe Riley Burns, Chairman
Division of Higher Education

AS LONG AS I can remember, the relationship of the Annual Conference to the college has, in the main, consisted of three things:

1. Providing money for operation
2. Recruitment of students
3. A vague, general review of program and policy.

The meetings of the Division of Higher Education have been so occupied with these matters there has been no time for a careful, structured study of deeper concerns. This week, for the first time, the Division has met on a college campus, not to transact business, but to ask ourselves serious questions about the meaning of higher education in the life and work of the church.

Why is the church in the business of higher education? What are our goals? What ends do we seek? Until we know the answers to these questions, we have no yardstick by which to measure the light of our success or the depth of failure. Our purpose is Christian education; but immediately we are faced with the question, "Why is a college Christian?"

Is it Christian when it is founded, owned, and controlled by the church? When it has a strong department of Bible and Religion? When the faculty is selected on the basis of Christian commitment? When it maintains regular and compulsory chapel services? When there are rules against smoking, drinking, and dancing? When the student body is drawn largely from church-family backgrounds?

Perhaps some of all these things. Yet something more. The role of a Christian college has to do with the *purposes* for which the college exists, with its *goals*, its *ideals*, its *intentions*. Perhaps it is best expressed by the often-used phrase, "Education of the whole man." It is found in that something extra which is added. It is education—*plus*!

The word is excellence. We strive for excellence in all things—excellence in the mind, the body, and excellence in the soul. Excellence for the whole man. Excellence is the kind of life our graduates will achieve, and excellence in the kind of work they will do.

Jim Gardner expressed it well when he said that we must have excellent plumbers as well as excellent philosophers. Otherwise neither our pipes or our philosophy will hold water.

The Christian college was never more needed than now. We live in an age that grows increasingly secular — secular in deeds, in words, in thoughts. To help build a society based, not on the secular, but on Christian principles, this is the task that confronts the church and all of its educational institutions.

Dennis Akin
Assistant Professor of Art

An aspect of wisdom is being developed on this campus—this aspect being reflection. And if I sense the faculty mood, it is that we are in the midst of the early stages of change by which we hope to discern more relevant ways to cause the acquisition of reflective knowledge that could ultimately lead to wisdom I trust that in some reasonable manner we shall be able to construct a program that will help "the student attain a reasoned framework of belief." Dr. Colwell, Dr. Wicke, and Dr. Pattillo have helped us open the door to a finer academic panorama.

85

THE PRESIDENT'S PAGE

"A GREAT college is a living, human, and growing thing. It is a web of personal relationships, permeated by a sense of dedication and loyalty to the *best* in life. Students and faculty recognize that to imitate each other is suicide; and to become jealous is just another form of ignorance. Real living takes place on such a college campus. Here is honest inquiry—joy—growth—development—enthusiasm—love—admiration—and hope. We seek to become strong liberal arts colleges—and that's fine. We also seek to be Christian colleges—and that is excellent. But, how are the two related?

The liberal arts attempt to *"humanize"* the race—while Christian higher education seeks to give *"reason"* for the liberal arts. When the highest quality of the liberal arts is given *purpose* and *illumination* by Christianity at its best—and when a campus is *moved* and *motivated* and *inspired* by a faith in the Christian scheme of things and commitment to God as the source of all truth—*there* you have Christian Higher Education in Action!"

C. Orville Strohl
President

THE SOUTHWESTERNER

Published monthly except July and August by Southwestern College, 100 College St., Winfield, Kansas. Second Class postage paid at Winfield, Kansas 67156

Why shouldn't a college campus, with imagination and uniqueness, do things of this kind every few years? It renews our dedication and builds morale.

87

The following are _excerpts_ from my reports to the Annual

Conference. I include them because they give a running account of our

programs and insights regarding approaches made.

1954

Bishop Dawson and Members of the Central Kansas Conference:
    When the Trustees of Southwestern College invited me to become
the President of Southwestern College they placed in my hands a very
sacred trust. I am humbly gratified for your confidence and for the
privilege of serving in a spot where there is such wonderful opportunity to enhance the lives of our youth.
    Our work at Southwestern College is nothing less than a part of
God's redemptive plan for the youth of this bewildered generation.
There is a big place for a Christian Liberal Arts education in todays
world. By the Grace of God and the prayers and devotion of His
people, your college at Winfield must become nothing less than that.
    Every time I walk across that 40 acre campus, I feel like I am
walking on sacred ground. The long hours, days, weeks, months and
years that have been given by those who have gone on before me -
remains a constant challenge. I am so grateful for their labors
and for their insights into the problems of human nature and higher
education.
    On Founders Day we launched a great 75th Anniversary program
that will bring us to our 75th birthday in 1960. In that program
we propose to do the following:
  1 Retire the $300,000. building program note.
  2 Launch an intensive student recruitment program.
  3 Strengthen our faculty.
  4 Build a new residence for men.
  5 Build a new President's home.
  6 Develop a chapel in the Administration Building.
  7 Finish the Administration Building - balcony in auditorium and
    lower floor.
  8 Campus Development and beautification.
  9 New Fine Arts building.
 10 A new girls residence.
 11 Organizing alumni groups and Southwestern College Associates.
 12 Underwrite the current budget each year.
 13 Increased dining room facilities.
 14 Increase the endowment.
    Together we can continue to grow and become! It is God's
Plan - and the people's deire.

88

1955

Bishop Dawson and Members of the Conference:

It is always a high honor and privilege to present the report for Southwestern College to the ministers and laymen of the Central Kansas Conference.

Southwestern College is entering her 71st year of continuous service to the youth of the Middle West, and especially to the Methodist youth of this conference. We have had many glorious records of achievement in the past, but I think none could exceed that of the year just past. The student body gave expressions of the Southwestern spirit through national achievements in music, debate, forensics and athletics. The morale of our students has never been higher than at the present time. The members of the freshman class of this year have been carefully selected and are of superior quality. We have over 40 students on our campus who are transfers from junior colleges. Students from other countries include India, South America, Mexico, Greece, Iran, Japan and Sweden.

Three young men from our student body attended the American University through the Washington Seminar. Professor Haywood is the chairman of this committee, and reports that these young people found the program valuable in training and practical citizenship. Southwestern is the only college in Kansas with this relationship with the American University-

We are making every effort we can to bring to Southwestern a group of housemothers who will be the kind of people that you would want your sons and daughters to live with in dormitory life. We have been exceedingly fortunate in our selection. Mrs. Saville and Mrs. Ross, both of whom are well known to many of you, are now occupying these important places of responsibility on our campus.

I drove out through Eastern Kansas early last spring, just after we had wonderful rains. It was early in the morning. The dawn of day had just begun. As I drove to the top of a hill, the view that greeted me from the distant valley was one of beauty and expansion. I was inspired! That's the way I feel about my job. The opportunities to serve our generation keep expanding before us, challenging those of you within the church to serve.

The 75th Anniversary Program stretches out before us, encompassing the dreams, hopes, and ambitions of the Board of Trustees and the faculty. In just a little less than five years from now, we will be observing our 75th birthday; It is our prayer and deepest hope that Southwestern College may be one of the strongest Christian colleges in the Middle West. It is God's will and the people's desire, and with our cooperation we shall move forward to fulfill this responsibility.

89

1957

One hundred and nine seniors graduated in 1957. The Hon. J. Ernest Wilkins, President of the Judicial Council of the Methodist Church, and Assistant Secretary of Labor of the Eisenhower Administration, made the address.

Bishop G. Bromley Oxnam will be the Smith-Willson lecturer in October. Bishop Oxnam will speak five times. Laymen, ministers, as well as friends of the college are cordially invited to avail themselves of any or all of these lectures. We are looking forward to this experience with high anticipation.

1958

The Board of Trustees have recently formulated an important statement of policy, part of which reads as follows: "American leadership, and indeed our national survival, is being challenged as never before. The survival and well-being of this nation depends as much upon the strength of Christian higher education as upon the strength of our military. Colleges in our democracy are expected to meet the fundamental needs of society. Responsible citizens share with educators a moral obligation to insist upon wise and careful planning to meet basic needs and to protect our institutions from hysterical demands and panicky reactions."

"When our institutions of higher learning are weakened, democracy, freedom, and the whole American tradition is threatened. The informed citizen is a valuable asset in a democracy where the majority make important policy decisions. The church related college represents a philosophy of western civilization which has been hewn out of the great moral and political ideas of religion and democracy. Our Christian culture depends upon colleges, free from the domination of government, that will teach that both religion and freedom are important to our survival. All our human resources must be vastly strengthened through the medium of improved Christian higher education."

It is against this background that we endeavor to express our dedication and commitment to Christ, our Lord, as we seek to guide and inspire a faculty, a student body, and a board of trustees, whose singular aim it is to build a great Christian college.

Public events at Southwestern College are planned to interpret to the public the things for which we stand. Christian leadership is one. The 1958 Commencement linked together the yesterdays and todays, and became a demonstration of the leadership of Southwestern's graduates. Dr. Roy L. Smith, distinguished graduate of 1908, inspired and challenged nearly one hundred seniors as they face their world in this great tragic hour of need.

90

During the year a very important decision was made by the
faculty and trustees. I refer to the change of membership from the
Central Intercollegiate Conference to the Kansas College Athletic
Conference. This takes us out of an athletic conference in which we
had membership for more than twenty-five years. It puts us into
competition with church-related colleges in Kansas whose purpose
and size are more equal to ours. This decision was made because we
wanted intercollegiate athletics to become a more integral part of our
academic program. This was a difficult decision to make because of
its nature. However, I am glad to say it was done democratically,
and all of us stand solidly behind the decision. I am proud that we
can make difficult decisions in a Christian spirit when such are
needed.

1959

We are not asking you to waste your money or time by investing
it in an educational institution that imitates secular colleges
and universities. At Southwestern we are concerned about students
coming to know Christ as well as Chemistry, and that they come to know
God as surely as they come to understand geology. The future not only
belongs to those who know, but to those who have an understanding,
appreciation, and commitment to Christian values.

1960

I have the honor to make the 75th Anniversary report for
Southwestern College to the Central Kansas Conference. It was the
church that gave Southwestern birth and nurtured her across these
many years. Southwestern has returned to the Conference and to the
world-wide church both lay and ministerial leadership. Our many
graduates are scattered all over the world and occupy places of
leadership in science, medicine, education, religion, business, law,
geology, literature, etc. Beyond their chosen professions, they serve
their communities both locally and nationally. Truly Southwestern
College is:

> "Old enough to have proven her worth and to have
> justified the vision of our fathers who established
> her and to the many who have invested their time and
> money in her behalf."

91

Slowly there has been emerging from the shadows the outline of a strong Christian liberal arts college. Southwestern is as important today in this great new expanding century as she was 75 years ago, when Kansas was a territory, and our nation was struggling to emerge into a great democracy. This anniversary year will see Southwestern's campus becoming one of the finest and best equipped anywhere.

The University Senate of the Methodist Church (the oldest accrediting body in America) made a survey of Southwestern's entire program. That report has been made to the faculty and trustees. Out of this 200 page survey will come the "Great Issues" that confront Southwestern in the next five or six years. These will become the heart of our development program.

New program developments include the establishment of courses in the Russian language, a Child Development Center as a third step in the Home and Family Life Program within the program of Home Economics.

Southwestern's Anniversary Program still includes two great events:

  a. The Anniversary Commencement, May 28-29. Dr. Elton Trueblood
     speaks both days on subjects relative to the development of a
     Christian college.
  b. The Fall Homecoming and the Smith-Willson Lectures. Dean Howard
     Thurman from Boston University is the speaker for the lectures,
     November 9-12.

Anniversary Birthday Parties are being held from coast to coast. Already hundreds of alumni and friends are visiting the campus. All of you are welcome during this special year - especially next fall during the Smith-Willson Lectures and Homecoming. All the new buildings will be open to the public.

We believe that in the providence of Almighty God Southwestern College is destined to face, with humility, but with courage, the unheralded future as a great Christian liberal arts college.

1961

On the eve of our 76th Anniversary Founders Day the trustees and faculty spent an evening with Bishop Slater and his Cabinet. Together we thoughtfully and prayerfully looked at the "Larger Tasks" facing Southwestern. In brief they are:

  1. To develop within Methodist laymen a moral and philosophi-
     cal dedication to the cause of Christian higher education.
  2. To challenge the church to make a universal commitment to
     Christian higher education.
  3. For Southwestern faculty and administration to understand
     that mere education is not enough.

A deep moving spirit gripped us. Out of this "new life" a stronger and more effective college is emerging.

92

1962

Special Features in 1962:
1. Exchange program established with Spelman College, Atlanta, Ga.
2. Students attend American University, Washington, D.C., each semester.
3. Dr. Yuen Zang Chang, Ph.D., is teaching a course in Chinese culture.
4. Miss Elaine Evans, junior, is attending the University of Vienna for one semester.
5. Introduction of a foreign language in our general education requirements. The languages taught now are Russian, French, Spanish and German.
6. Southwestern College, in cooperation with seven other colleges, has now established the collegiate tours of Europe. Several students will travel in Europe in the summer of 1962.
7. Mrs. Billie Day (1960) is teaching in a Methodist Girls School in Africa, having gone by way of the Peace Corps.
8. Dr. Ralph Sockman was the Smith-Willson lecturer for 1961. Bishop F. Gerald Ensley will be the lecturer in 1962.
9. Three Sunday evening vespers were held this year, the preachers being Dr. Ronald Meredith, Dr. Douglas Jackson and Dr. Ralph Sockman.
10. Southern Rhodesia project supported by friends and churches as we seek to provide education for leaders of our church from Africa. These young people will be on our campus for three more years.

Special recognition has come to our Board of Trustees as our President, Mr. George Templar, has been nominated and appointed by President Kennedy as a federal judge. Judge Templar will continue as President of the Board of Trustees. He will be our Commencement speaker, Sunday evening, May 27, at 6 p.m. This kind of Christian leadership is of importance and we take renewed hope because of it.

In deep gratitude to each of you, and to Southwestern's many friends, and to God whom we all endeavor to serve, may I express my appreciation. I renew my dedication to the task of Christian higher education as Southwestern seeks to fulfill it.

1963

In the midst of many philosophies of higher education and the great national debate as to what America's commitment should be to higher education - Southwestern stands taller and stronger as a Methodist related college in the great midwestern belt of America - free from the domination of government. Southwestern knows that facts are not wisdom until they are related to spiritual values.

93

One ought to raise the question as to whether or not all the struggle and sacrifice for the building of a Christian liberal arts college like Southwestern are justified! But why would Southwestern want to be anything less or anything else? This is big business in partnership with God! All the gifts, sacrifices, and devotion of former generations for a Christian college are at the mercy of those who are now in responsible positions. We declare that their dreams and sleepless nights shall not have been in vain.

The General Conference asked her church-related colleges to play a distinct role from that of secular educational institutions. Our hearts were warmed when Bishop F. Gerald Ensley, of the Iowa area said to me, and later confirmed by letter: "You are meaningfully making over Southwestern into the image of a church college. More power to you!"

We accept the challenge. With God's leadership and your cooperation and help, we shall endeavor to lead Southwestern forward in this desperate hour of human need to become a citadel of Christian hope, love, and learning.

1964

Our work is our love made visible as we continue to find new ways to make the purpose of Christian higher education a reality to the youth of our generation.

In the midst of the clamor for higher education across the land there is the "still small voice of God" both powerful and persistent, warning us of the dangers beset in much of higher education. This is especially true if it is just more of the same, and if it renounces its concern for a Christian interpretation of life.

Students are bewildered and seek to find some reason for their existence. The whole nation was bewildered at the time of the assassination of President John F. Kennedy. One would have thought that the great centers of learning (the universities and colleges) would have had some word for mankind.

Instead, governors asked the chancellors of the state universities to dismiss their classes. I know of no state college or university that did otherwise. But, many private colleges, including Southwestern, called their students and faculty together, and in a spirit of silence and worship, endeavored to look at the diminished stature of America, and asked for moral and spiritual reinforcements. Why should not higher education have something to say when the need is great? (A copy of this program, including addresses, was sent to Mrs. Kennedy. She returned a letter of appreciation to Dean Haywood.)

An educator from the University of Alabama, not from the little villages back in the hills, but from the university campus, said recently that thousands of Americans in the South are frightened by what is happening. They are frightened not merely by the terror, physical struggle, hatred, and revenge - if they take a stand - (these are bad enough); but what is even more frightening, is the development of a split mind, a dichotomy of the mind. The wilderness and the jungle are at hand.

94

Why does not higher education speak to this terrifying situation? The answer is that most of higher education is secular.
Higher education based on a secular philosophy has no lifting power
to elevate morality and redeem human life. In secularism there are no
absolutes; facts are separated from values, and values from power.
There is no vision of an ideal, no understanding of an irresistible
power to which life can be commited. There is no place for self-
sacrifice.

These ingredients are found in Christian higher education.
Nothing short of a scholarly and Christian mind can ever solve
these deeply-rooted problems of our time. The need for Christian
higher education of a new dimension is the most pressing problem of
our decade. A college can gain the whole world and lose its own
soul. I pray that Southwestern may be saved from such an error.

The story of David and Goliath is being repeated. I am convinced with vigorous and creative imagination that this Annual
Conference, linking its energies with its colleges and the eternal
resources of God, will continue to build God's Kingdom throughout
the world.

I am glad to be counted one with you in this great enterprise.

1965

The basic problem of our generation is the struggle to preserve
the Christian concept of man. No segment of the earth has escaped its
effects, and no institution can avoid its problems. The church-
related college is especially involved because the struggle concerns
our basic philosophy of higher education.

All the money that is spent, the classes that are taught, the
buildings that are built, the students who are recruited, and
endowment money that is invested, is done so with the hope and
prayer that our program in the Christian liberal arts will set our
students free so that they will join their fellowmen in this great
undertaking.

Southwestern must help in this struggle as much as is possible.
The future of the church is involved, democracy is at stake - indeed
all of Western Civilization - if not the whole world.

On March 2, 1965, the Wichita Eagle gave Southwestern a full
page entitled, "80 Years Old and Still Growing." A fine editorial
appeared in the same issue entitled, "They're Small But Great."
In these 80 years, hundreds of our graduates have achieved greatness.
In just a few days, this will be in evidence again as General D.C.
Strother, a Four-star General in the United States Air Force, will
return to Winfield and the campus, where he was a student, to deliver
the commencement address. General Strother has been the United
State's representative to N.A.T.O., and has just recently been
advanced to Commander of the North American Air Defense Command
(N.O.R.A.D.). Commencement is May 30, 1965, at 6:00 p.m.

95

1966

The Smith-Willson Lectures in October brought together Christian
leaders who participated in seminars, workshops, and lectures with
students, faculty, trustees, ministers, alumni and friends of the
college. Out of these experiences came the publication entitled
"A Sense of Direction." The following four items were highlighted:
(1) The place of the Christian scholar on the campus; (2) The place
of religion on the church-related campus; (3) The college as a
Christian community; (4) The relationships of Southwestern College
to the church.

The Board of Trustees appointed a Steering Committee and charged
them with the responsibility of working out a five-year program
for Southwestern - 1966-1971. The work of the Steering Committee
has been brought to our faculty and to a special meeting of the
Board of Trustees held on Monday, April 25.

1967

ACADEMIC BLUEPRINT

This far-reaching study and revision began two years ago and was
released to the public under the title of "A Sense of Direction."
The program has now been formalized and will begin in September,
1968.

The "Southwestern Idea" basic to this new program, reads as
follows:

Southwestern College is one of the few liberal arts schools in
the United States which, having examined its relationship to the
modern world, has determined to make a thoroughgoing revision of its
curriculum.

One of the most evident changes which is being proposed is the
new organization of the school year calendar. The new calendar will
have three terms, fall, winter, spring. The fall term will begin
early in September and run fifteen weeks to the middle of December.
The winter term will be a short four-week term in the month of
January. The spring term will be a fifteen-week term beginning in
February and running to the end of May. Of particular interest is
the short winter term which provides an opportunity for presenting
those topics which should have the total concentration of the student's
effort directed toward the single goal.

The aim of the new curriculum is to give the student a functional
command of his field rather than a mere accumulation of facts.
To this end, the emphasis will be on understanding rather than
root learning. Each discipline will also pay particular attention
to its relationship to other departments of learning.

96

1969

1954--FIFTEEN YEARS OF PROGRESS!--1969
SOUTHWESTERN COLLEGE. . .

DREAMED!
    DARED!
        FACED DANGERS!
            ACCOMPLISHED

WHAT SHE SET OUT TO DO IN 1954!

The Master Plan included 13 new buildings--38 acre expansion
of the campus--a quarter-mile cinder track with 220 runway--and a
3½-million-dollar addition to the endowment, a new academic blue-
print, and an enrollment of 700 students.

THIS HAS NOW BEEN ACCOMPLISHED!

The college has continuously operated in the black--by hard
work and the cooperation of thousands of donors. Therefore with
the Master Plan completed before construction costs had advanced
so rapidly--and no nagging deficit to liquidate ...we are continuing
to--

G R O W
in depth, in quality, and in purpose!

Southwestern College has never had as great a challenge--and has
never been as well prepared with faculty, students, trustees, plant,
endowment, and administration as today.
    The new program for the 70's entitled--

"COMMITMENT TO ACHIEVEMENT"
is designed to help us to BECOME!

Southwestern is not a custodian of the old order, a perpetuator of
the proven, or a curator of the present. This college is an open-
ended venture, selective of the past, a creative critic of the pres-
ent--and oriented toward the tomorrows. She is not only a creature
of society, but must help create a new society,

ALL ONE CAN DO WITH LIFE IS RISK IT!
WE INVITE YOU TO RISK IT AT THIS PLACE
AND AT THIS TIME.

97

1970

Thomas Carlyle admired his father for two things--tough-mindedness and deep devotion. His father was crude and unculti-vated, but the Christian religion "made him and kept in all points a man."

That's the goal of Southwestern College--to inspire, assist and motivate our students so that they will become "in all points real men."

One year ago Southwestern set forth on a five-year program known as "Commitment to Achievement." The program is designed to deepen and enrich the academic life of our campus and to increase the endowment by six million dollars.

It was the part of wisdom to have completed our $6,000,000 educational plant in 1968. (Today it would cost $10,000,000.)

It was carefully planned to have a total new academic blue-print for 1968-69, which has proven to be most effective through the last two years even though some revisions are always essential.

It was educationally sound to gather together a strong faculty oriented toward the Christian liberal arts.

We are thankful for a dedicated and knowledgeable Dean of the College.

The Beech Aircraft Foundation established the Olive Ann Beech Chair of Business Administration in September, and are underwriting it with an initial gift of $100,000.

Our beloved W. W. Monypeny, who was associated with Southwestern for 35 years, died on the eve of Southwestern's 86th Founders Day. Fifty-seven (57) percent of his estate comes to us to endow two scholarships--one in memory of Kate, his wife, and one in his name. He said, "I still want to be associated with the college that I so deeply loved after I am gone."

1971

I am convinced that the greatest experimental program of the United Methodist Church is taking place on her college campuses.
Here we find a value system related to all facets of life in the 20th century.
Here we find reconciliation taking place in numerous areas between races, between generations, between secular and religious ideas, between people where understanding and tolerance are needed.
The interpretation of the meaning of human existence in different disciplines takes place daily. This relates itself to the steward-ship of the air, soil, water and other natural resources.
When our students discover ultimate purpose for their human existence, they have discovered the key by which to live.
This is Southwestern's purpose. All that we do must contribute to this end.

98

This is the third year for our new academic program. Its
effectiveness continues to grow. The emphasis is now upon:
    Individuals rather than groups
    Inquiry instead of memory
    Excitement for learning rather than a spiritless climate
    Team teaching
    Interrelatedness of knowledge through Foundation courses.
    We have moved away from classrooms like kitchens to ones like
libraries and living rooms, from teaching to learning, from non-
participation to involvement of students in their own education,
and from all textbook learning to some first hand experiences.
    A new graduate program is being started this summer in conn-
ection with Oklahoma City University known as "O.C.U. at Southwestern
College." Five courses will be given leading to the M.A.T. degree.
    We look upon this relationship as a sustaining one - and
hopefully it will be broadened in months ahead.
    Dr. Stephen White, Ph.D. in Physics from the University of
California at Riverside, was our commencement speaker. He is a native
Kansan and a Southwestern graduate.
    The Rev. Paul Hagiya of Denver, minister at Simpson United
Methodist Church, and also a graduate of Southwestern, preached
the baccalaureate sermon. His topic was "Reconciliation is a
Beautiful Word."
    Rev. Hagiya graduated from Southwestern in 1944. He was a
displaced Japanese-American. This was during the war and the rise
of hatred toward the Japanese. On his way to Winfield he tells
how difficult it was to find food, even a hamburger. Mrs. Deterick,
house mother, took him in and fed him. The City of Winfield objected
to his being on campus. Mr. J.J. Banks, President of the Chamber
of Commerce, was very vocal in his opposition. The college stood
by him and he graduated. He became a very effective minister in
the Colorado Conference of the Methodist Church. He served on
several city-wide commissions on Race in the city of Denver. He
also served on some national commissions.
    When he returned in 1971 to the campus, it was a very moving
experience for him and for us. He is an excellent preacher. On
that occasion, J.J. Banks sat on the front row and, following
the baccalaureate sermon, was the first one to put his arms
around Rev. Hagiya and tell him how wrong he had been in those
years of 1940-1944. This made his sermon theme a reality.

1972

    This is my nineteenth and last report of my stewardship of time,
energy and effort as President in behalf of Southwestern College.
Therefore, I will set forth some basic and philosophical beliefs
upon which our program is developed.

99

In 1885 Methodists in the southwestern section of Kansas selected Winfield as the location of their college. Through the years they have maintained a deep interest in her strength and vitality.

At the same time, the college has maintained at the center of its purposes a concern for the sharing of its spiritual search, for an honest confrontation regarding the ultimate issues of life, and for a wholistic reconciliation of the claims and insights of religion and science, of faith and reason.

There never has been any effort exerted by Methodists that Southwestern should be sectarian. From the beginning, young people of every race and creed, who were qualified for college, were welcomed to her campus.

Southwestern College, from a hilltop on the edge of Winfield, has built strong links over many generations, and around the world, with other cultures and nations. Her program reaches to the national capitol in Washington, to the United Nations in New York, to the Pacific and India, as well as to Europe and Africa. Her summer program in academic studies is founded at the University of Graz in Austria. Her graduates are now living in 21 countries. They are serving in responsible positions as career diplomats, educators, government leaders, and in foreign affairs. The January Term sees our students in many states and, over the years, in many countries.

As Southwestern moves into the 70's, she rests her case upon certain convictions about the nature of man and his destiny in a global culture. The base upon which she operates includes the wide range of educational, spiritual, and social concerns. These cluster around the Judeo-Christian value system that becomes the heart of man's stability, confidence and outreach.

Our graduates become "decision makers." Decision makers must know how to think. Our wide-flung program in debate, our quality program in theater, and our in-depth programs in the natural sciences, language, fine arts, and the social sciences are all pointed in that direction.

Southwestern College is not a custodian of an old order, a perpetuator of the proven, or a curator of the present. This college is an open-ended venture selective of the past - a creative critic of the present - oriented toward the tomorrows. The ultimate validation of Southwestern's program is to be found in the competence of her graduates.

In a survey made by the National Academy of Sciences, entitled "Doctorate Recipients from United States Universities - 1958-1966," it was revealed that Southwestern College produced more graduates who received the Ph.D. and Ed.D. degrees than any private college in Kansas over a 45 year period. This does not include those who earned doctoral degrees in Medicine, Law, and Theology.

100

Not only did Southwestern College rank first in Kansas, but rated high amoung such colleges as Earlham (Indiana), Grinnell (Iowa), and Macalester (Minnesota). Students were chosen Woodrow Wilson Scholars in the Senior Classes of 1968, 1967, and 1966. Thirty-five to thirty-seven percent of Southwestern's senior class are accepted by graduate schools each year.

The effort to maintain Southwestern's program as described above has become a very great and acute responsibility in the decade of the 70's. It is as hard for a non-tax supported (and non-profit) institution of higher education to live through a period of inflation and economic instability as it was for a family to have lived through the depression of the 1920's and the 1930's. Remember those days!

Southwestern Has Been Diligently Preparing for the Future:

Her endowment has been increased by 3½ million dollars. It is now $4,300,000. Each year these permanent investments produce over $200,000, which is used for operating costs of the college. Each year this endowment principal is increased from gifts and bequests. Southwestern seeks to increase her endowment to ten million as soon as possible.

Her plant is completed for the 70's. It is valued at $9,570.251. We are not plagued with high construction costs.

Her new academic program is now moving into its fifth year and has been accepted by students, faculty and alumni with enthusiam.

Her faculty is dedicated, committed, and well prepared to share their lives with our students who come from 24 states and a number of countries beyond our own.

Her students are friendly, genuine, wholesome, and academically qualified for collegiate life.

PART FOUR

TO FASHION A DREAM

101

TO FASHION A DREAM

William James once said, "The greatest use of a life is to spend it for something that outlasts it." Sidney Harris has said, "We possess nothing except what we have shared or given away. We are all part of the great chain of life, and we must forge stronger links, not break them."

On the cover of this story is a church steeple and the College seal. These three symbolize our rural background, the place that a christian faith had in our lives, and the influence of college life. Helen and I chose to spend our talents and life in the ministry of the church and the church related college. As I prepare this statement on the eve of our 50th Wedding Anniversary, I have nothing but deep gratitude for what these years have meant to us.

On page 16 of this book I outlined 3 areas which I considered to be basic in anyone's life. They are - One's profession - One's lifestyle - One's life companion.

This is where our dream started (1933) and, after half a century, we look back - and report on our stewardship. These 3 factors (work, faith, love) become tightly interwoven and support each other like the strands of a rope. So, my comments are unified with singleness of purpose.

First, it isn't everyone's fortune to have these three factors equally strong. And, even if they become strong, it doesn't just happen. A couple must work at it, and we did, with joy!

102

Second, for two people to "love and cherish" each other for over 50 years is a miracle! Our hearts kept tugging at the same load. Sylvia Morris, biographer, (Edith Kermit Roosevelt) says, "Devotion shapes history. The relationship between husband and wife is absolutely vital in understanding a presidency." Daniel Boorstein, Librarian of Congress, says, "Presidential character and personality often affect history as much as policy decisions." I understood this, and when the college committee invited me to receive The Moundbuilder Citation in 1972, I requested that Helen be given one at the same time and place. They are now framed together in my study.

Third, for two people to share the joys and woes of a tough job--where hours are long, where travel is involved sometimes for many days, where income is limited--and vacations are uncertain--is also a sign of deep understanding and love of two people.

Fourth, the love and grace of God has added strength to our lives and given us a sense of joy in our work. Helen & I hold our marriage as a sacred and wonderful relationship. Neither of us could have asked for more.

Our family consisted of three children whose names and dates of birth have been recorded earlier. But here they are again...

        Sheryl Jeanne - February 1, 1937
        Helen Joanne - May 28, 1941
        Rodney Neal   - November 25, 1944

Our children have had good health and all of them have acquired a college education. They have faced their usual problems of growing up --and often times "Preachers Kids and "Prexies Kids" felt they were a bit singled out.

103

There were times of great concern on our part because parents always suffer even more than their children when their problems arise. And we did. We have learned, I think, to be patient, to try to understand, not to panic and remain loyal in love. As parents we have always felt that our children had a right to know how we felt about their problems, and many times our suggested solutions were far from their own. Through the years all 5 of us have had the same closeness as we have always had. In that relationship we have had fun, far more than the usual family. A highlight in December of 1978 was our trip together to Hawaii for the Christmas holidays and we look forward to our trip together to Seattle and Victoria in the summer of 1983.

We have welcomed whole heartedly two sons-in-law and a daughter-in-law into our family circle. They are Dorothy Elaine, Gary Alexander and M. Lynne. These 6 people, who mean so much to us, are actively engaged in the church. In addition, we are grateful that they are family centered, community minded, and occupy places of great responsibility in their work... Southwestern Bell Telephone, International Business Machines and the Phoenix Gazette.

Our nine grand children are...

    Cyndy Diane Clark Johnson
    Kimberly Jean Clark
    Caroyln Chris Clark
    Stephanie Joanne Clark
The 4 above are Sheryl's children.
    Todd Gregory Strohl
    Rodney Brian Strohl
    Chad Owen Strohl
The 3 above are Rodney and Dorothy's children.

104

Kirk Alexander Darfler

Elizabeth Lora Darfler

The 2 above are Joanne and Gary's children.

Fifty years to shape the dream of a considerate, compassionate family of 15 provides us with great joy. It is our deepest hope that the 3, the 6, and the 9 will always remember our family heritage, the things that meant most to us, and that our memories will be an inspiration to them.

Not only will our children and grand children outlast us, our work has been crowned with unusual success and will continue to outlast us for years unlimited. The three churches we served in the 30's and 40's are stronger than they have ever been, the Iowa churches and her college have gained great strength.

The most enduring work of our hands has been Southwestern College. In 1972 we completed that beautiful campus--a picture of which in included in this book. We undergirded it with an endowment which has now grown to 11 million dollars. I can think of nothing that is more important to the youth of all generations and to the life of the church than a strong Liberal Arts College.

I cannot explain how such a turn-a-round could have taken place for the college. It was far more than hard work. It was more than a tenure of 18½ years. I know of no reason why we should not recognize that God, working through many people, clothed our simple ways with grandeur and success and created a college that stands at an all time high.

 SOUTHWESTERN
COLLEGE
WINFIELD, KANSAS

105

Fifty years ago such a dream was far beyond our comprehension. I do recognize that having graduated from Southwestern has been an asset. It provided me with an inspiration. It gave me an acquaintance with many alumni, former faculty and a general knowledge of the region. As we look back upon these years we are not only proud, but humble and grateful.

Through these 50 years we were guided in almost a mystical way. Each step we took we gained strength for the next. Good pastorates laid the foundation. Then teaching on the college level in two colleges, Drake University and Iowa Wesleyan, assisted. State wide experience in Iowa for a decade. Wide acquaintances and seeing four church related colleges at work in Iowa. Yes--"lead kindly light"--all was taking place without our knowing what the next step or challenge might be. Then after 20 years we were called to our alma mater. I couldn't have had a richer or more varied background of solid preparation within the confines of the church. There are those who say we saved Southwestern. So let it be!

Being a college president demands an unusual combination of talents. History has revealed this to be true. Trustee search committees looking for a new president have an awesome task. They need to remember that their new College President will have to work with a very wide spectrum of people. He works with 2 generations at least. Students are our main purpose but older people are essential to help finance their needs. There are faculty and faculty are different than anybody else. There are alumni, trustees, ministers, laymen, townspeople, corporations, foundations and the leadership of the Church on the regional and national levels. There are other College Presidents who always wonder if you are going to get ahead of them.

106

I have always said that we, Helen and I, had just enough success
to keep us _encouraged_, and just enough failures to keep us _humble_. In
the Geta, the sacred writings of India, one finds these words: "He is
not elated by good fortune nor depressed by bad. Such is the Seer."
Really, the college President one sees on special occasions, dressed in
robes and hoods, is not, by any means, the real President. The real
President wears "overalls" and work clothes and is not a race horse but
a _plow_ _horse_. The bottom line, however, is can he raise money? Big
money! Those who give that kind of money want the President involved.
And, once it is given, they want it used intelligently. If it is not,
watch out!

For my successor I didn't leave an aspirin box with a note (see
page 46) saying "Good Luck" I left a memorandum, a part of which said,
"The greatest concern I have is for the Corporate life of Southwestern
College as an institution. In my estimation, the stronger Southwestern
becomes as an institution, the greater advancements we can make in all
related areas. Unless the "Center" is strong, no other part of our
program can have strength. This has been a guiding principle in my
administration through the years. It has given rise to the thought
by some that I was more concerned about the institution than I was
about persons. This has not been true. I know that persons will wither
and disappear if the institution to which they are related is destroyed
through neglect and mismanagement."

"The forces that work against this Corporate life are a strong pull
away from definite institutional goals, purposes, and dreams. Each
group wants to "do their own thing", and yet they want the institution
to do more for them."

107

"Thus I have always felt that my task was to keep "energizing"
the staff -- guiding them toward common goals -- and sometimes lowering
the boom, when necessary."

"I would continue to require deliberation regarding basic decisions.
Hasty decisions are not good. (Easy Street is a dead-end street)
Southwestern's trustees and administration especially are known from
having made sound decisions in the past. The intelligent use of our
resources, including money, is a very important impression to be spread
abroad among our donors and friends."

"I have tried hard to keep the campus from cliques among faculty,
administration and students. There is a strong tendency for academic
people to ignore the non-academic--for student leaders to ignore the
less active students, etc. I feel that all faculty and administration
people should be included in academic affairs, academic processions,etc."

"Because of this conviction we usually have had an all-campus meeting
in the Tri-Dining Area in January or early February with some kind of a
report or talk concerning the direction of the campus."

"If I had it to do all over again, I would continue to try to stop
all end-runs that are being made--or when one is tempted to make an end-
run. I would also be very cautious about students playing one office or
one administrative person against another. Students are noted--as well as
faculty--for doing this sort of thing."

"_A strong Board of Trustees_. These men and women who give of themselves
and their money and of their time for very little appreciation shown them by
the faculty and students--and that is the reason I think it is so important

IN RECOGNITION
OF 18 YEARS
OF DEDICATED SERVICE AND
LEADERSHIP
TO SOUTHWESTERN COLLEGE AND TO
THE MANY STUDENTS
AND OTHERS
SERVED.

Announcing

The
Orville and
Helen Strohl
Endowed Scholarship Fund

AT SOUTHWESTERN COLLEGE

for the administration to show some appreciation for them. You have heard me say--and I think it is absolutely true--that an institution like a college or university goes no farther than their Board of Trustees is willing to lead them."

"Formula for recovery and advancement, a copy of which is attached. Together we share the risk. If faculty, students, and administration could realize that together with the Board of Trustees we must share the risk for tomorrows, it would be a real accomplishment. Small risks today at many points will result in larger gains for tomorrow."

Together we shaped a Dream!

P.S. Helen reminds me that in all our ministry we were never asked to terminate any assignment. We were always invited to accept a new position. The first such experience took place at Carlisle (see page 29). When we hear of trustees issuing one year contracts to Presidents we wonder what that means.

Statement From Alumni Board

The following statement regards the establishment of "The Orville & Helen Strohl Endowed Scholarship". The brochure sent to Alumni and Trustees is attached.

PART FIVE

THINGS THAT I HAVE LEARNED

109

PART FIVE

THINGS THAT I HAVE LEARNED

1.

In the play, "Tea House Of The August Moon" there is a closing statement made by an American soldier which I adopted and have used in my attitude toward my work. The soldier said -- "I have learned to live between my possibilities and my limitations". I have found that there is great relief in doing well the things you can do - and have the good judgement not to do the things for which you have no talent. This saves much tension and frustration.

2.

"If a kite is to fly, it must have a tail to balance it". What does this mean? A decision might be proper - but the way it is presented - or announced will make all the difference as to how it is understood, and will be accepted. Things must look right, as well as be right. Every virtue must have a counter virtue. Freedom is a virtue, but it must be balanced with responsibility. One can illustrate this in many ways. It works!

3.

We learn from negative experiences as well as positive. Reflect upon them and ask oneself, "What did this mean?". "What can I learn from it?" Read between the lines. I have referred to some experiences of this nature above.

4.

Judgement! Never make hasty decisions. Quick decisions on major matters are usually dead-end streets. Hang up ideas to dry, so to speak.

110

Look at them tomorrow or next week. Get other peoples ideas, listen objectively and then decide. Cultivate this virtue and before long it will be easier to make sound judgements. I heard Pat McConnell years ago tell about the stone mason who built a beautiful fireplace. But when the fire was lighted it smoked because it didn't have the proper draft. Poor judgement on the part of the mason. Poor judgement usually results in smoking fireplaces.

5.

Appreciation and Gratitude. Thomas Aquinas said, "Whatever is received, is received according to the recipient." Genuine appreciation, thankfullness and gratitude for the smallest acts of kindness as well as the larger ones is so basic.

I decided, while at New London, Iowa that I would never let anyone come to my church study and leave without saying something that would be inspiring, encouraging or express my gratitude to them for something that they had done. Why don't we do more of that? It is needed and it works wonders. Even the worst negative person responds and we have created a stronger friendship.

6.

Never panic. Be like a duck--remain calm on the outside but paddle like the dickens underneath.

7.

Authority is like a bank account. The more you use of it, the smaller amount you have left. And sooner-or-later you are bankrupt. Use it carefully, wisely and only when it is really needed.

111

8.

Water seeks it's level. The historian has said, "The mills of God grind slowly but they grind exceedingly small." Ones inner motives and thoughts eventually will be in control. "As a person thinketh so he becomes."* That which gets your attention finally gets you.

9.

"Do not think more highly of yourself than you ought to think." (Romans 12:3) Couple this with Gandhi's statement (age 23-1893) "It has always been a mystery to me how men feel themselves honored by the humiliation of their fellow beings." If a person has confidence in himself then he won't always be the victim of others--rather he will be the victor. He is guided by an inner strength and serenity and peace and joy that far outweighs any circumstance that might arise.

10.

Hard work and long hours is seldom enough to win. There must be a strategy--a way, a method, a plan. The same strategy will usually not work the second time because every situation is different. However, all problems can be solved if we give them deep thought, careful analysis and constant effort.

11.

Never worry who is going to get the credit.

12.

Team work is an art. It engenders excitment, creativity, new ideas, will power, and commitment.

* Proverbs 23:7

112

13.

Never get used to the average. It is so easy to settle down to the acceptable. The fortune teller who said to the lady, "I see nothing but poverty, struggle, fear and unhappiness in your life - and then at 40?" "What at 40?" she asked. "Then you will get used to it".

14.

Every person needs a tear bucket and a cheering section. Helen has been mine. Someone to listen, to encourage and to be there when needed. In the book of Ephesians, one is advised never to go to bed angry. I have had no problem with that. It's staying up all night that has bothered me. (tongue in cheek)

15.

Share success with those with whom you work. Very often someone standing in the shadows has had a crucial part in your victory. President Mossman of Southwestern, during his first term as President, spoke far and wide about the successful program underway on the campus. But there was a very wonderful man on campus by the name of Prof John Phillips. Prof John was the President's counterpart. Mossman never understood how important Prof John was until Mossman moved to Morningside College in Iowa. He did the same amount of field work but the campus never responded as it had in Winfield. He didn't have a Prof John on campus to put his ideas to work.

113

16.

Successful people (strong, busy) in high places are usually approachable. This has been very revealing to me. They respond to challenge and need. Eleanor Roosevelt did when I got acquainted with her. Arthur A. Smith, Vice President of the First National Bank of Dallas, did and became a trustee and close friend.

17.

Friends are kind when personal problems emerge in life. Our family did not escape them - but by the Grace of God - we tried to remain humble and survived them. Do not try to explain or deny them. Be honest.

18.

Little people become great when they link their lives with great purposes.

19.

Do not worry over having too much to do. A creative person is like that. And most tasks could be done better if we had more time. This is a good point of view because it helps during years of retirement.

20.

We have learned to recognize the young. It's enriching to do so - for often, younger people are ignored.

21.

Try not to be judgemental at any stage in life. But especially as one grows older.

22.

Compassion - only humans possess the capacity for it. On December 25, 1918, in a "little house on the prarie in Meade County" Mother gave to Eugene and me a copy of Daniel Defoe's book - Robinson Crusoe. During

those long and lingering December and January evenings, Mother read to us
the story of this adventure.

I can see her yet. Seated by the kitchen table, kerosene lamp by
her side, she read to Dad and the two of us. I became so concerned
about the hero of the book. Robinson Crusoe was lost on that little
island. He needed food, shelter, companionship and, most of all, someone
to help him find his way home. I was inspired, moved and I asked questions.

Something happened to me during those quiet evenings. The flame of
"compassion" was awakened. I had no idea that this "Virtue" was so basic
to life. And certainly it is essential in the life of a minister.
Webster defines compassion as " consciousness of others' distress -
together with a desire to alleviate it, to sympathize".

Administrators who are effective need an abundance of compassion.
Think for a moment how essential this virtue has become as one works
with students who are having problems and faculty who are stuggling.
Extending this feeling into all areas of life, third world nations,
foreign students, etc., one sees how essential compassion really is.

Sixty four years later, 1983, at Christmas time in Denver, Joanne
pulled down from her library some books that we had given Sheryl years
before. Sheryl had given Joanne these books before she moved to Phoenix,
Arizona. One of them was Defoe's Robinson Crusoe. On the inside fly
leaf, in my mother's handwriting, are these words - "Orville and Eugene
Strohl - For Christmas - 1918". I treasure that book and will keep it
always. My mothers gift to us is enough. But beyond that she read it
aloud and it awakened and nurtured a basic emotion by which all people
live. Compassion is also a word from the New Testament and is found
often in the life and teachings of Jesus.

115

23.

The Magic of Moral Leadership. On page 58 of "Gandhi, Soldier of Non-Violence," the author says, "The people of South Africa had never seen a man work so hard or so unselfishly. His earliest followers said they loved him even if they didn't understand him." The implications are startling! Humility, devotion, dedication to a cause with singleness of purpose laced with love and truth will break through to others where nothing else will. We are misled so often in thinking that degrees, skills and cleverness will get the job done. They won't!

24.

Establish policies and then operate on them. The quickest way to create confusion and uncertainty amoung those with whom we work, is to operate out of "your hip pocket." Policies should be widely known so that no one is caught off guard.

25.

An administration will be asked to accept or support ideas and/or programs that they do not fully understand. Have them fully explained and think them over, or do not accept them until you have a "gut feeling" that you can support them.

26.

If the right people meet for the right purpose at the right time, wonderful things can happen.

27.

Stewardship is using money for the right purpose at the right time for the right cause.

116

28.

Leave some projects unfinished so that those who pass by may see vividly where their help is needed.

29.

Exposure becomes the point where we learn. To expose oneself to the best, greatest, or neediest keeps one alive, alert and fresh.

30.

I learned that a president is often over-exposed to the faculty and students. It is equally as bad to be under-exposed. To always be around or never to be available is a fine line to observe. The balance is basic.

31.

The word is integrity. Without it our credibility is challenged and it becomes the beginning of the end.

A FINAL WORD

I started with a quotation from William James and Sidney Harris about the greatest use of a life. That quotation is, <u>the greatest use of a life is to spend it for something that outlasts it. Death cannot destroy that kind of a life and partnership</u>!

I also have referred to our immediate and ever enlarging family and how closely knit we are in a beautiful and helpful way. Two great historians, Daniel Boorstin and Sylvia Morris, both biographers, have recently released a study in which they conclude that, <u>Devotion Shapes History</u>. Helen and I see this <u>spirit of devotion</u> in and through our family, reaching on to our Grandchildren, and we are confident that such devotion of <u>parent and child</u> will extend for generations to come. Without devotion to <u>ideals</u>, to <u>dreams</u>, to <u>each other</u>, to <u>God Himself</u>, life is pretty barren.

For a full life -

Do more than <u>touch</u> - <u>feel</u>!
Do more than <u>look</u> - observe!
Do more than <u>think</u> - ponder!
Do more than <u>read</u> - absorb!
Do more than <u>hear</u> - listen!
Do more than <u>listen</u>- understand!
Do more than <u>talk</u> - act and become!

- <u>This we bequeath to generations of our family</u>

<u>to come</u>!

PART SIX

HISTORICAL BACKGROUND OF SOUTHWESTERN COLLEGE

<u>A NARRATIVE</u>

<u>THE STORY OF SOUTHWESTERN AND THE BUILDER IDEA</u>

Southwestern College was founded in 1885. A committee of seven men was appointed by the Methodist Annual Conference to find a suitable location for a college campus. The hill overlooking the Walnut Valley appealed to them because of its natural beauty and the vision that it made possible. It later became the locale of <u>The Master's Degree</u> by Margaret Hill McCarter. She referred to Southwestern as "Sunset College". Her novel has caught something of the romance and the pioneer spirit that characterizes our Alma Mater.

Methodism's first college was established in 1785. It was named for two Methodist pioneers—Francis Asbury and Thomas Coke—Cokesbury College. In 1960, Southwestern's 75th anniversary, I had the following <u>inscription</u> placed on a hugh 8 ton bolder that had been taken from the side of the hill where the College and Student Center is built. It links Southwestern with Cokesbury College. It reads as follows: "Methodism founded her first college 9 years after the Declaration of Independence was written and 2 years before the Constitution was framed. The year was 1785. One hundred years later (1885) Kansas Methodism founded Southwestern College. For 75 years Southwestern has kept her <u>vision</u>, <u>pride</u> and <u>integrity</u>".

Southwestern's second building crowned this hill, and for nearly sixty years has been the center of the campus. The original building had a lighted dome that became a landmark. It could be seen for miles from all highways. A new building completed and dedicated in 1956, is now floodlighted at night. The four pillars at the entrance of Christy Administration Building have stood since 1905. They stand for <u>knowledge</u>, <u>hope</u>, <u>courage</u>, and <u>freedom.</u>

Beyond the four pillars the "77" steps lead to the lower campus. These steps have become the famous "77". Freshmen scamper up and down them in delight as they become acquainted with Southwestern. Seniors march up them in all the dignity of an academic procession at commencement time. These seventy-seven steps have helped to develop a deep sense of loyalty and dedication to their Alma Mater.

Bishop Alfred Quayle, standing at the top of the "77" once said, "God could have made a more beautiful view, but he never did".

Florence Cate, inspired by the view at the top of the hill, wrote the words of "The Alma Mater":

Far above the Walnut Valley,
On a lofty height,
Stands our noble Alma Mater,
Bathed in golden light.

Far above the stir and bustle
Of the busy town,
Reared against the arch of heaven,
Looks she calmly down.
(Chorus)

To the heights she calls us daily,
Alma Mater dear,
Heights of knowledge, hope and courage
Free from doubt and fear.

Lift the chorus, speed it onward
Over hill and dale,
Hail to thee, beloved Southwestern,
Alma Mater, Hail.

The "Building of the Mound" was inaugurated by Dean Leroy Allen in 1927. It dramatizes the Southwestern spirit. This ceremony gave rise to the name "Moundbuilders". The name has been used widely. The "Builder Spirit" is referred to by all students on the campus and by many thousands of our alumni. It catches up into a popular phrase the purpose and spirit of Southwestern.

The Builder Spirit is very real. It lays emphasis upon individual worth, the power of discipline, the redemptive quality of Christian fellowship, and the need for faith in God as the ultimate reality that gives meaning and purpose to human existence. It has been, and is a fighting spirit. It is a contagious spirit. It engenders enthusiasm and hope, loyalty and dedication, sacrifice and cooperation.

THIS, THEN, IS THE GOAL WE SEEK!

We seek to develop a campus where dignity, freedom, and responsibility become contagious. Where new buildings, kept clean and neat, become functional and useful for our purposes of Christian higher education. Where a campus stateliness creates an atmosphere of culture and good taste.

We seek to provide our students the best of education in the liberal tradition.

BUILDERS BELIEVE - that there are extraordinary possibilities in ordinary people--
that if we throw wide the door of opportunity to every boy and girl who is
willing to assume their own responsibility for their education -- we will
get amazing results.

BUILDERS BELIEVE - that young people will develop with responsibility.

BUILDERS BELIEVE - in the informal values of higher education. Therefore
students are requested to become a part of the campus community by living in
the residences, eating at the dining hall, and sharing creatively in the work
and responsibility of a college campus.

HISTORICAL BACKGROUND

THE COLLEGE HILL AREA

In the office of the Register of Deeds in Winfield is a copy of a declaration of ownership of a tract of land made by the College Hill Town Company. The tract on College Hill is fully described giving the names of streets and avenues. The tract lies just East of College Street, extending from Simpson Avenue as the South boundary, to Fowler Avenue as the North boundary. The tract extends four blocks eastward with Stevens Street as the eastern boundary. All of the tract was pictured as having been laid out in city blocks, with subdivisions of lots shown, excepting the part between Warren and Fowler Avenues and between College and Houston Streets. This portion, the equivalent of six city blocks, is marked as a location for the Methodist college. The date of the recording of the declaration of ownership was July 22, 1885. It was signed by Tom H. Soward, President of the College Hill Town Company, and Charles H. Bantage, secretary of the company.

Evidently there had been some understanding, prior to the date given, relative to the location of the college since that section was not laid out in town lots.

Also in the office of the Register of Deeds is a copy of a warranty deed, dated August 18, 1885, just 27 days after the recording of the declaration of ownership mentioned above. The deed shows that the area mentioned as not being laid out in city lots was transferred to the "South West Kansas Conference of the Methodist Episcopal Church" in consideration of the location of the "South West Kansas Conference College". The document shows the property was deeded by the "Highland Park Town Company".

It is not clear how this tract, owned by the "College Hill Town Company" on July 22, 1885, could be deeded by the "Highland Park Town Company" 27 days later. The transfer of property is no doubt recorded some place.

On May 23, 1888, the First College Hill Addition was recorded. This tract was east of Stevens Street, extending three blocks farther east and from Simpson Avenue on the south to Fowler Avenue or farther on the north. The avenues were extended from the first described tract and streets were laid out and named. Evidently this first addition was never settled for early in the 90's all streets and avenues were officially vacated.

The sheet attached hereto shows the property referred to above with the names of all streets and avenues shown. It has been the declaration for many years that the streets and avenues bear the names of former Bishops of the Methodist Episcopal Church. Investigation reveals that all of the avenues have the names of Methodist Bishops. Included are Simpson, Ames, Janes, Warren, Ninde, Bowman, and Fowler. Ninde and Bowman Avenues, lying between Warren and Fowler, no longer exist. As has been stated, the portion in the First College Hill Addition has been vacated, and this portion in the tract bounded by Houston and Stevens Streets is now part of the college campus.

There is no evidence that the streets running north and south were named for bishops. Soward was probably named for Tom Soward, president of the town company. The only streets bearing names of bishops are McCabe and Vincent. Both of these served as bishops later than the dates mentioned with descriptions of tracts.

A brief statement concerning each bishop named is given below:

(1) Matthew Simpson: East & West
        Served as a Methodist bishop from 1852 to 1880 according to the
        disciplines for the years mentioned.

(2) Edward R. Ames: East & West
      Named as a bishop from 1852 to 1872.

(3) Edmund S. Janes: East & West
      Named in disciplines from 1844 to 1872.

(4) Henry W. Warren: East & West
      Listed in disciplines from 1880 to 1908. Later was co-founder of
      Iliff School of Theology, Denver, Colorado.

(5) William Ninde: East & West
      Listed from 1884 to 1900. In 1884 he was the resident bishop in
      Topeka, Kansas. "Closed as campus expanded".

(6) Thomas Bowman: East & West
      Shown as serving from 1880 to 1912. "Closed as campus expanded".

(7) Charles H. Fowler: East & West
      Served from 188r to 1904.

(8) Bishop McCabe: North & South

(9) Bishop Vincent: North & South

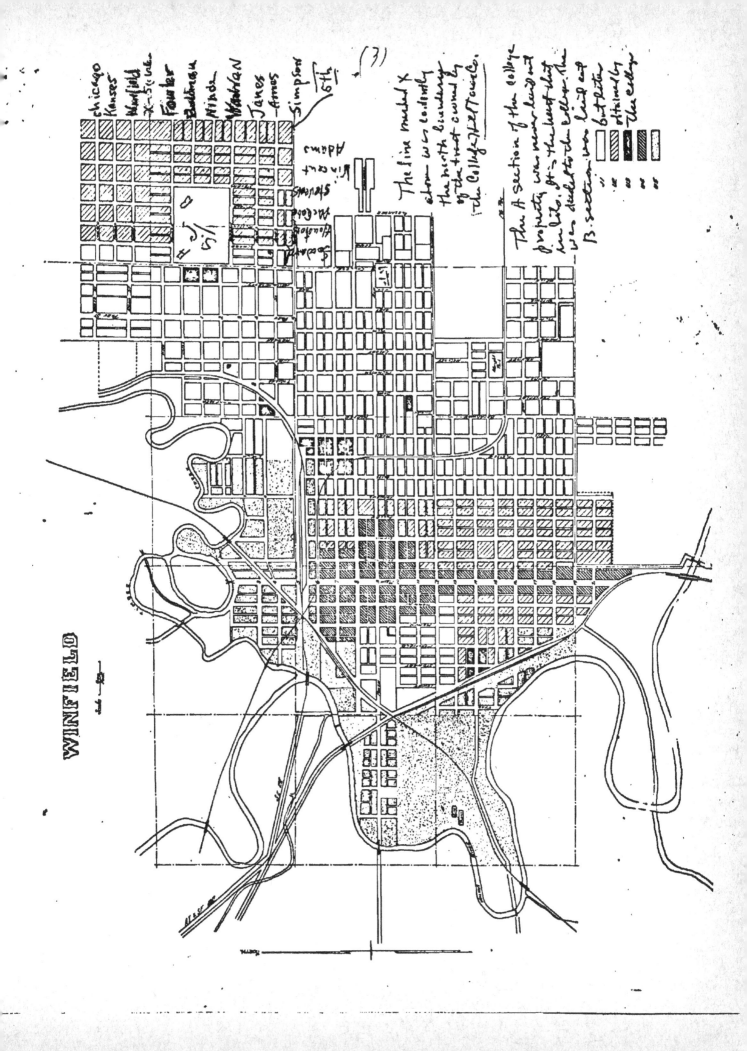

IMPORTANT DATES   1885-1985

March 23, 1885	Resolution of the Southwest Kansas Conference of the Methodist Episcopal Church to organize a college within its bound
June 19, 1885	Charter issued to the Southwest Kansas Conference College.
1885	The city of Winfield pledged 40 acres of land, $60,000 in cash, the stone for the erection of a building, the free use of water for the work, and all of the lumber and hardware at cost.
April 20, 1886-1890	John E. Earp assumed the Presidency.
Sept. 1886	The original college building, Old North Hall, opened for use.
Sept. 7, 1886	Opening day of school for Southwestern College.
1887	Erection of the President's home.
Fall of 1887	A three story frame ladies' boarding hall was completed.
June 3, 1889	Degrees conferred on the first graduating class of the college, numbering three.
June 11, 1890	Milton E. Phillips assumed the Presidency.
1894	William N. Rice assumed the 'acting' Presidency.
1894	Granville Lowther assumed the 'acting' Presidency.
Jan. 3, 1895	Chester A. Place assumed the Presidency.
1899	William H. Rose assumed the 'acting' Presidency.
April 11, 1900	Fred C. Demorest assumed the Presidency.
Oct. 1, 1901	Charter ammended to increase the number of trustees.
June 4, 1903	George F. Cook assumed the Presidency.

1908	The erection of original gymnasium, a frame building East of the Presidents home, dubbed 'Prexy's Barn' by the students.
Aug. 8, 1905	Frank E. Mossman assumed the Presidency.
1918	William R. Ward assumed the 'acting' Presidency.
1909	Contract for the erection of Richardson Hall let for $62,000.
July 19,1909	Charter ammended, changing the name of the college to Southwestern College.
Dec. 6, 1911	Charter renewed for fifty years.
1914	The University Senate of the Methodist church rated the college in class "B".
1915	Southwest Kansas Conference voted campaign for $600,000, of which $200,000 was to be for sustentation and $400,000 for endowment.
Nov. 29,1916	Launching of campaign for endowment that resulted in reaching a goal of $678,000.
March 1917	Southwestern College became accredited by the North Central Association of Colleges.
Jan. 1, 1919	Albert E. Kirk assumed the Presidency.
1920	Erection of Smith Hall, a dormitory for women, named for Mr. and Mrs. Irvin Smith of Kinsley.
Summer 1922	Summer school inaugurated.
1923	Conversion of old Y.M.C.A. house into a dormitory for women, originally called Huss Hall, but later changed to East Hall.

March 15,	1923	Letting of contract for Stewart Field House for $132,490.
Nov. 15,	1925	Launching of campaign for $1,750,000 for debt-payment, endowment, new equipment for Southwestern College and student work at the tax supported state schools of Kansas.
Oct. 21,	1928	Ezra T. Franklin assumed the Presidency.
December	1930	Granted full membership in the National Association of Schools of Music.
March	1931	Southwestern was dropped from the accredited list of the North Central Association following internal dissention resulting in the resignation of President Ezra T. Franklin, and at a time when the college was temporarily without a president.
	1931	R.L.George, pastor of Grace Methodist Church, assumed the Presidency.
June 1,	1931	Frank E. Mossman assumed the Presidency for his second term.
March	1932	Southwestern College was re-instated on the accreditation list of the North Central Association.
October	1934	Conference approval of a program to secure $278,000 to pay all outstanding indebtedness and launching of that program.
	1938	Installation of the Kibbe Organ, the gift of Mr. Henry Kibbe of Winfield.
October	1939	Southwest Kansas Conference and the Northwest Kansas Conference merged to form the Central Kansas Conference of the Methodist Church, which Conference had two colleges, Southwestern College and Kansas Wesleyan University within its bounds.

May 27,   1942-44   Charles E. Schofield assumed the Presidency.

October   1943   Board of Education report affirming the policy of
                       continuing both colleges as Conference colleges adopted
                       by the Conference.

May 1,   1945-49   Mearl P. Culver assumed the Presidency.

             1947   Erection of the Sonner Stadium, a gift of Mr. P. J.
                       Sonner of Winfield.

Summer of   1947   Student Union, Music Hall, Wesley Hall (Men's residence
                       hall) and Married Students' apartments erected on the
                       campus from buildings given the College by the U. S.
                       Government at a cost of $160,000.

             1949   Raymond E. Dewey (Acting)

September   1949   North Hall condemned by state fire marshal.

October 17, 1949-53   Alvin W. Murray assumed the Presidency.

April 16,   1950   Richardson Hall burned precipitating the discussion of
                       the question as to conference policy concerning the con-
                       tinuing of two colleges, after which a special session
                       of the Central Kansas Conference was called for June 29,
                       1950 "to consider matters pertinent to the program of
                       Southwestern College."

June 29,   1950   Special session of the Central Kansas Conference at which
                       time a resolution to create a commission to bring a plan
                       for merging Southwestern College and Kansas Wesleyan
                       University to the next regular session of the Conference
                       was defeated by the vote of 241 to 98 and the Million
                       Dollar Building program of Southwestern College was endorsed
                       without a dissenting vote.

August 31, 1950		Contracts let for Construction of Mossman Hall of Science.
September	1950	Contracts let for construction of Memorial Library.
September	1950	Plans to raise $150,000 "in the clear' within the Southwestern zone.
June 15,	1953	P. J. Sonner organ installed.
	1953	Raymond E. Dewey (Acting)
	1954-72	C. Orville Strohl elected President (Began Jan. 1, 1954)
	1972-79	Donald Ruthenberg
	1979	Forrest Robinson (Acting)
	1980	Robert B. Sessions
	1985	100 years of continous existence.

SOUTHWESTERN'S HISTORY ON A PAGE ~

SOUTHWESTERN COLLEGE, WINFIELD, KANSAS, ~ FOUNDED 1885 ~ CALLED THE SOUTHWEST KANSAS CONFERENCE COLLEGE UNTIL 1908 WHEN THE NAME WAS CHANGED TO SOUTHWESTERN COLLEGE ~ FIRST CLASSES MET IN McDOUGAL HALL (Down town and rented) SEPTEMBER 7 1886

ORGANIZATION				ENROLLMENT									DEGREES		
Year	President	Buildings erected	Endowment	Liberal Arts	Fine Arts	Academy	Normal	Business	Miscellaneous	Total	Repetition	Net	Liberal Arts	Fine Arts	Honorary
1886	Edw E Earp	North Hall													
1887				112	94			73		279	50	229			
1888				111	86			113	(2) 30	301		340	3		
1889				110	59			69		238		238	3		
1890	McLean Phelps			No Record											
1891				25	28	124	56	34	(1) 37 (2) 40	344	33	311	2		1
1892				57	208	185	103	56	(3) 35 42	686	173	513	5		
1893				107	155	269	64	214	(4) 71	880	267	613	3		1
1894				No Catalogue published this year									7		
1895	Chester Pace			27	136	107	18	36		324	115	209	4		
1896				23	96	83	39	28	(3)(2) 2 3	274	26	248	7		
1897				24	135	118	32	40	(5) 1	350	81	269	4		
1898				21	103	134	34	62		354	50	304			
1899				29	95	118	48	87		377	63	314	9		
1900				35	53	87	33	86		294	17	277	7		
1901				40	145	109	28	98		420	134	286	4	2	
1902				46	151	99	42	110	(4) 13	461	152	309	5		2
1903				45	183	92		105		425	161	264	8		
1904				48	220	117	58	133		576	85	491	10	1	2
1905				43	287	106	60	126		622	180	442	11		2
1906				58	109	121	52	62	(5) 16	418	47	371	13		
1907				88	153	138	69	101	(6) 17	566	99	467	12		1
1908				97	226	133	74	111		641	136	505	16		
1909		Richardson Hall		126	260	158	81	95		720	168	552	10		
1910			49,969.81	135	237	169		90	(6) 15	648	158	488	16		
1911			58,829.31	178	175	157		102		612	151	461	25		
1912			60,791.81	196	145	138		59		547	135	412	23		
1913			63,219.68	229	196	130		55		610	150	460	29		
1914			65,992.68	251	144	91		59		545	132	413	39		
1915			87,938.18	269	113	65		64		511	123	388	32	3	
1916			89,820.18	276	115	51		56		498	120	378	33		
1917				304	124	25				453	98	355	45	4	
1918	Wm Thoriel Ward		202,931.	258	114					372	72	300	28	1	
1919	Albert E Kirk		228,952.10	304	124					428	66	362	41	2	
1920		Smith Hall	256,887.28	429	212					641	156	485	16		1
1921			296,760.79	525	193	(SUMMER SCHOOL)			(*) 26	744	154	590	59	2	1
1922			312,012.	588	198	88			(7) 35	909	197	712	64	2	1
1923		Stewart Gym.	317,398.	726	252	105			(7) 39	1139	200	939	98	3	4
1924				718	214	214			(7) 12	1158	139	1019	109	4	
1925			330,077.66	736	327	245				1308	196	1112	113	2	2
1926			342,220.53	740	344	372			(7) 43	1499	335	1164	128	4	1
1927			359,806.91	730	528	369			(7) 60	1687	341	1346	118	6	3
1928	Earl T Franklin		439,784.37	671	246	543			(8) 40 222	1722	400	1322	113	7	2
1929															

* 1 Unclassified   4 Sub-Preparatory   7 Extension
  2 Primary   5 Post Graduate   8 Preparatory School of Music
  3 Selected Studies 6 Model School

Compiled by Wm. T. Ward, 84, Secretary Board of Trustees

PART SEVEN

FOR THE RECORD

PART SEVEN

FOR THE RECORD

1972-73 - <u>Sabbatical</u>. During the year we were delayed by a car accident

on July 3, 1972. Interviewed and offered a position at Illinois

College to raise money for a new library. Could not accept

because of Helen's broken shoulder.

1973   - <u>January trip to Mexico</u> and a visit with Christine Wolf,

Southwestern graduate. Visited international Girl Scout Center

and other historical spots.

1973-75 - <u>Associate minister at First United Methodist Church</u> in

Winfield. This has been my home church since 1923!

1975   - <u>Official retirement</u> from the Kansas West Annual Conference

on May 27.

1975-77 - Appointed to the <u>Commission on Governmental Ethics</u> on July 1

to January 31, 1977.

1974-75 - Chairman of the Bi-Centennial Commission for Winfield. Ten

persons on the committee. Activities included publishing a

history of Winfield and the communities in the Walnut Valley.

All day Fourth of July celebration, ending with a huge crowd

at Sonner Stadium for fireworks. Public schools and most of the

community organizations shared in the year long program. The

Memorial Park was named 'Independence Square' by the City

Commission for the year 1975. Special recorded music was

aired at intervals at the park. The Centennial flag was

flown in the park. Records of all the activities, the flag,

signs, seal, etc. are in the Cowley County museum.

1975-81 - Member of Four Winds Girl Scout Board of Directors, and
became treasurer within a year. Secured $12,500 from Kansas
Gas and Electric for scouting. Lease for oil on girl scout
ranch and it was a producer! Built a new Girl Scout Service
Center at Augusta in 1979, and moved the offices from El
Dorado at a cost of $85,000.

1978   - Appointed by the City Commission of Winfield to membership
on the board of trustees of William Newton Memorial Hospital.
Elected chairman in the fall of 1982. Appointments are for
a 5 year term, with possibility of re-appointment. Five
members on the board.

1976   - A special study tour of the area that was the Cradle of
Christianity (Egypt, Israel, Greece). John Trevor, student
of the Dead Sea Scrolls, Bishop and Mrs. James Matthews were
amoung the leaders of the study seminar.

1976-77 - Treasurer of the Political Committee of the 5th Congressional
District to elect Duane 'Pete' McGill as U.S. Congressman.
Result - No win!

1979-82 - Member of Conference Pension Action Committee of the United
Methodist Kansas West Conference. The goal was seven million
dollars to underwrite the pension program.

1959-79 - A member of the Bi-State Mental Health Foundation. Its offices
are in Ponca City, Oklahoma, and Cowley County is included.

1974   - Teacher of an adult church school class at First United
Methodist Church, whose attendance is maintained at an
average of 40.